USS LEXINGTON

DETAIL & SCALE'S FIRST VOLUME ON A SHIP

in detail & scale

Bert Kinzey

KALMBACH BOOKS

Airlife Publishing Ltd.
England

Copyright 1993 by Detail & Scale, Inc. This book may not be reproduced in part or in whole without written permission from the publisher, except in the case of brief quotations used in reviews. Published in the United States by Kalmbach Publishing Company, 21027 Crossroads Circle, P.O. Box 1612, Waukesha, WI 53187.

CONTRIBUTORS & SOURCES:

LTJG (SW) Jennifer Boyd, USS LEXINGTON
Photographic Section, USS LEXINGTON
Larry Gertner
Ray Collins
National Archives
Depart of Defense Still Media Records Center
U.S. Navy

Photographs with no credit indicated were taken by the author.

FIRST EDITION
SECOND PRINTING

Cataloging-in-Publication Data

Kinzey, Bert.
    USS Lexington : in detail & scale / by Bert Kinzey
      p.   cm. -- (D&S ; v. 29)
    Originally published Blue Ridge Summit, PA : TAB Books, 1988.
    ISBN 0-89024-172-4 : $11.95
    1. Lexington (Aircraft carrier : 1943-) I. Title.
[VA65.L4K56 1993]
623.8'225--dc20   93-1020
                                 CIP

First published in Great Britain in 1987
by Airlife Publishing Ltd.
7 St. John's Hill, Shrewsbury, SY1 1JE

British Library Cataloging In
Publication Data:
Kinzey, Bert
U.S.S. Lexington -- (Detail and scale series ; v.29).
1. Aircraft carriers -- United States.
I. Title II. Series
623.8'55'0973   U874.3
ISBN 1-85310-606-2

Front cover: The USS LEXINGTON is the last operational unit of the ESSEX class of carriers that were designed just prior to World War II, and were modernized in the 1950s. This is AVT-16 as she appears today during operations in the Gulf of Mexico. The photograph was taken in May 1987.

Rear cover: LEXINGTON's final World War II scoreboard is shown in this rare color photograph from 1945. Trophy flags for Air Groups 16, 19, 20, 9, and 94 are visible, as are tonnage figures for naval and merchant shipping. Kills and assists by the ship's guns are also included at right. Below the scores is a listing of all the actions in which LEXINGTON participated, and to the right of that is a total score for the LEXINGTON as of September 1945. The white ducks have numbers in them indicating the number of aircraft destroyed on the ground. Included in the totals are 387 aircraft destroyed in the air, 635 aircraft destroyed on the ground, 588,000 tons of naval vessels sunk or damaged, and 497,000 tons of merchant shipping sunk or damaged.   *(USS LEXINGTON)*

TO THE READER

This book on the USS LEXINGTON was written in late 1987, and first published in early 1988 when the ship was still in service as the U.S. Navy's training carrier. It is the end result of many hours of extensive and detailed research which was conducted in order to provide a detailed and accurate account of the ship's history in World War II as well as her service after she was recommissioned in 1955. Additionally, a very detailed account of her modernization and conversion to an angled-deck carrier is included. Hundreds of historical photographs were studied in order to select just the right ones that would illustrate the ship during her early service life and show the important physical changes that would interest naval historians, enthusiasts, scale modelers, and the general public.

During the preparation of this book, the author flew out to the LEXINGTON on three separate occasions in order to take photographs of the ship and the air operations that were conducted on her flight deck. Two more trips were made to the ship while she was in port to take detailed photographs of every part of the ship. In all, over 3,000 photographs were taken, and from these the photographs in this book were chosen.

With the exception of this page, this book remains as it was written in 1987 while the ship was still in service, but it continues to be the most detailed, accurate, and up-to-date publication available on the USS LEXINGTON. The carrier went on to serve in the training role as explained on page 29 until finally being retired from service four years later. She was replaced as the Navy's training carrier by the USS FORRESTAL. Fortunately, LEXINGTON was saved from the scrapper's torch, and she has been turned into a floating museum at Corpus Christi, Texas. Her records for the most launches and arrested recoveries will stand forever in the annals of Naval Aviation. It is also unlikely that any present or future carrier will ever equal her combat record. It is therefore fitting that many thousands of visitors now have the opportunity to learn about her records and service as they visit the world's most historic aircraft carrier.

INTRODUCTION

The USS LEXINGTON, CV-16, was the second aircraft carrier of the ESSEX class to be commissioned. Once in service, she participated in almost every major engagement in the Pacific from September 1943 until the end of the war. Only twice during that time did she return to the United States, once for repairs, and a second time for an overhaul. Because of the fact that she never was painted in a "dazzle" camouflage scheme, she became known as "The Blue Ghost." On four separate occasions the Japanese reported sinking her, which is quite an exaggeration, since only twice did she receive significant damage in combat. This photograph was taken as the ship prepared to launch a strike in April 1944. F6F Hellcats, TBF Avengers, and SBD Dauntless dive bombers can be seen on the deck. (National Archives)

The first twenty-eight volumes in the Detail & Scale Series were all on some of the most famous aircraft in aviation history. In Volume 29, the USS LEXINGTON becomes the first ship to be the subject of the familiar Detail & Scale format. The announcement that ships would be included in this series was met with an enthusiasm that was even better than expected. But a few people questioned why the LEXINGTON was to be the first ship covered. Those who asked this question thought that a modern nuclear-powered carrier such as the USS NIMITZ (CVN-68) or the USS ENTERPRISE (CVN-65) might be a more fitting choice. While these supercarriers may well be the subjects of future volumes, the LEXINGTON clearly should be the first ship to be included in the Detail & Scale Series.

Most students of U.S. Naval history would probably select the first carrier ENTERPRISE (CV-6) as the most significant aircraft carrier in history. But certainly the USS LEXINGTON, which was launched as CV-16 on June 16, 1942, is a close second. She has served the United States longer and has set more records than any other carrier in the history of naval aviation. Known as "The Blue Ghost," her service record in World War II was exceeded only by that of the ENTERPRISE. Then, completely modernized, she began her post-war service in 1955. Today she remains the only ESSEX class carrier in service. She has been designated CVA, CVS, CVT, and AVT during this post-war period. As this book is written, LEXINGTON is closing in on her 500,000th arrested landing, a record that undoubtedly will never be equaled by any other carrier. Her starboard catapult has recorded almost 300,000 launches, the most by any catapult on any carrier. Although she has been scheduled to be withdrawn from service several times, present plans probably mean that she will see her fiftieth birthday still in service with the U.S. Navy. When she is finally decommissioned, the LEXINGTON will have served the United States longer in war and peace than any other carrier, past, present, and most probably future. Her records for landings, launches, and miles steamed will probably stand forever in the annals of naval carrier aviation. This is why the LEXINGTON should be the first book about a ship, and this is best summed up by her final World War II score card as illustrated on the rear cover.

Research for this volume was begun with some degree of concern, since every book that could be located on aircraft carriers (including one on LEXINGTONs, CV-2 and CV-16) mostly used the same photographs over and over again. This seemed to indicate that there may be little in the way of photographs available for this publication. But a trip to the National Archives and to the Department of Defense Still Media Records Center turned up several thousand photographs. Over one hundred were selected for possible use in this book. Additionally, two trips were made to the LEXINGTON while she was conducting flight operations in the Gulf of Mexico. Over 1500 photographs were taken during those two trips. Still more photographs were taken on a third trip that was made while she was in port. Many of these photographs show the details that are the emphasis of the Detail & Scale format. They will provide the modeler with valuable assistance in building an accurate model of the LEXINGTON. The photographic section aboard the carrier provided additional pictures. In the end we had a large quantity of photos to select from, and very few of the photographs in this book have ever been published before. For the most part, we have kept the narrative to a minimum, making every effort to include as many of these photographs as possible. These pictures and their captions tell the story of the LEXINGTON. They cover the

Captain H.G. "Woodie" Sprouse chats with the Air Boss during a lull in flight operations, May 1987. Seen between them is the starboard catapult of the LEXINGTON which has recorded more launches (close to 300,000) than any other catapult on any carrier in the Navy. (Collins)

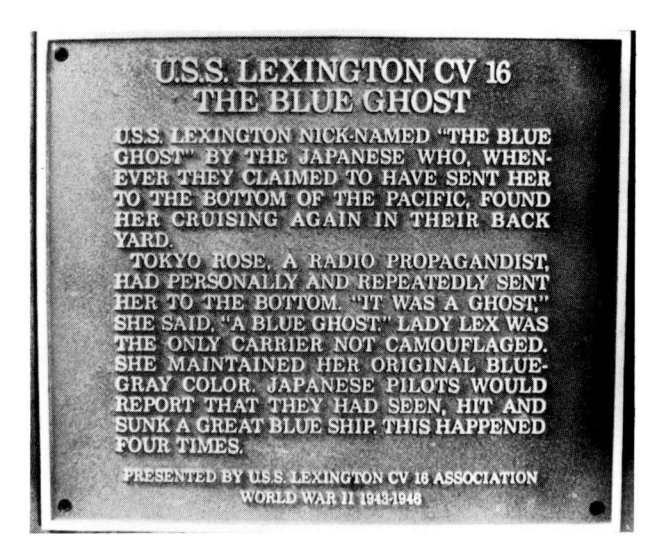

The USS LEXINGTON CV-16 Association placed this plaque on the ship, and it remains there today. It explains how the nickname "The Blue Ghost" was given to the carrier. During most of the war, the USS LEXINGTON was painted in Measure 21, overall Navy Blue, which accounts for the "great blue ship" that the Japanese pilots reported seeing. Other carriers of the ESSEX class, most of the INDEPENDENCE class, the ENTERPRISE, and the SARATOGA all had the "dazzle" camouflage schemes at one time or another. After her April-May 1945 refit, she was painted in Measure 21, a graded system of Navy Blue or Navy Gray up to the hangar deck, and Ocean Gray from there on up.

ship's design details, combat history, modernization, air operations, and post-war service. There are over twenty pages showing details of the ship as she appears today.

Photographic coverage was not the only area where we were fortunate. Detail & Scale was provided the complete official World War II history of the carrier taken from the ship's files. Although long since declassified, the original still bore the SECRET classification from the war years. This history was used to write the text for the carrier's operations in World War II. This text provides important information and dates on all of the actions in which the LEXINGTON participated between her commissioning in February 1943 and her return home after VJ day.

While many members of the ship's crew were most helpful, a special thanks is deserved by LTJG (SW) Jennifer Boyd, the Public Affairs Officer aboard the LEXINGTON. Her efforts in providing assistance and information went far beyond simply doing her job. Much of the credit for any success that this book attains belongs to her. She is directly responsible for providing access to take many of the photographs and for obtaining much of the information presented on the following pages.

Our Modeler's Section includes information on the best way to build a model of the LEXINGTON as she appeared in World War II and in her post-war angled deck configuration. We are pleased to have Larry Gertner, well known for his ship articles in IPMS/USA publications, write about how to build the ship as she appeared in World War II.

Many people visit the LEXINGTON each year while she is in port. They see the plaques that have been placed where a suicide pilot crashed his aircraft into the ship, where a torpedo hit the stern, and in the hangar bay where the names of the LEXINGTON's shipmates and aircrews that gave their lives for their country are listed. It is a sobering and solemn experience. Anyone with a sense of patriotism and naval history cannot help but reflect on the gallantry and heroism that took place on the decks of this great ship. In peace, more naval aviators have landed on her flight deck than on any other carrier. In 1958, the USS ENTERPRISE, CV-6, was ordered scrapped, an act that, in the opinion of this writer, was nothing short of criminal. Hopefully, when the days of service are finally over for the LEXINGTON, she will be spared the same fate. It would be fitting for her to be placed on permanent display near the Naval Aviation Museum at NAS Pensacola, Florida. No aircraft carrier will ever again serve this country in both war and peace for so long a time. To scrap the LEXINGTON would be to destroy a part of history, and this must not be done. Detail & Scale is proud to present this book as our first title on a ship. In this way we hope to help preserve part of the history that belongs to "The Blue Ghost."

DEDICATION

U.S.S. LEXINGTON CV-16
THE BLUE GHOST
WORLD WAR II
SHIP'S COMPANY

HAROLD E. ANDERSON, S2C
GERALD J. BARRIER, S2C
WILLIAM C. BEATON, S2C
J.W. COLEMAN BECK, S2C
HAROLD E. BERRY, S2C
GERALD H. BIRD, MUS2C
ROY W. BLACKWOOD, S2C
OTTO C. CARTER, S2C
LT. JOHN H. CLIFFORD
WILLIAM E. CLINGERMAN, QM3C
PHILIP C. COLEMAN, Y1C
RICHARD E. COOK, S2C
LT. COMDR. LANE O. COSS
ROBERT S. CRAMER, S1C
JAMES F. CROWELL, Y3C
JOHN F. CULLEN, AMM2C
MYRAN P. DEAN, CSKP
RONALD D. DEMOSI, STC
REAL E. DUBOIS, TMV2C
FRANCIS E. FOSTER, SM3C
EUGENE E. GILBERT, JR. S1C
WILLARD H. GRIEBEL, AMM1C
EDWARD HANTON, STM1C

CHARLIE A. HOLT, S1C
WILLIAM A. HOURIGAN, S1C
ARTHUR C. HUNTON, S1C
WALTER W. IRVIN, JR. S1C
WALTER J. KALESKY, S1C
THEO KIPP, AMM3C
IRVING KLEIN, S2C
ROBERT L. KLEMECKE, S1C
RICHARD W. KLUVER, S1C
EDWARD J. KRAGE, S2C
JOHN J. LIBOUREL, AERM3
JAMES J. LILES, S2C
VICTOR R. LIUZZI, JR. S1C
JAMES H. LOCKHART, S2C
THEO L. LONG, S2C
ENS. FRANK J. LYONS
ROBERT M. MAGGI, S1C
ELMER M. MATULIS, ARM2C
FRANCIS X. MC CABE, S1C
LT. GEORGE J. MELVILLE
CARL W. MERRITT, COMGQ
EDWARD E. MIKITY, FC2C
WILLIAM M. MILLER, QM3C

DONALD E. MITCHELL, S1C
WILLIAM MITCHELL, SM3C
SAM H. MOATES, GM3C
WENDELL T. MOFFITT, SM3C
SERGEANT A. NELSON, PHOM1C
JOHN A. NISBIT, QM3C
KIMSEY A. PATTERSON, S2C
ALBERT C. PION, PFC USMC
LAWRENCE M. PRENDERGAST AOM3C
JAMES REED JR. STM1C
TOMMY A. SAMPLES, S1C
WARD E. SEYMOUR, S1C
WILLIAM T. SINS, ACMP
LEONARD W. SMIGIELSKI, EM2C
CORNELIUS R. SOPER, COX
MARCUS A. SPANN, S1C
ERVIN W. STANTON, S1C
TRUMAN C. STEWART JR., S1C
THOMAS B. STICKNEY JR., FC3C
CHARLES W. TAYLOR, SK3C
RICHARD C. THORN, S1C
JOHN E. WASHKUHN, SK3C
JOSEPH C. WASSUM, F1C

AIR GROUPS
AIR GROUP 16

LT. WARREN H. ABERCROMBIE
LT. LEROY F. ARMSTRONG
LTJG. GUILFORD F. BRANSON, JR.
LT. MARK K. BRIGHT
ENS. HOMER W. BROCKMEYER
ENS. THEO A. BROWN
LTJG. WILLIAM E. BURCKHALTER
JAMES E. CAREY, ARM1C
ENS. THOMAS CARLISLE
JOHN T. CLEVENGER, JR. AM2C
GEORGE W. COUGHLIN, ARM3C
LT. ROBERT O. CURRY
LTJG. PAUL DANA
LTJG. FRANK M. DELGADO
DAVID L. DELLINGER, ARM1C
LT. WILLIAM E. FITCH
GENE R. GREVO, SEA2C
HARRY R. HADDEN, JR. AMM1C
LTJG. EDWARD L. HEACOCK

COMDR. ROBERT H. ISELY
GEORGE J. JOHNSON, ARM2C
LTJG. RICHARD G. JOHNSON
ENS. WILLIAM N. JOHNSON
ALFRED O. JUNGMEYER, ARM2C
LTJG. JOHN D. KENNEY
ENS. NILE C. KINNICK
LTJG. NEWBOLD R. LANDON
LEO O. LEMANY, ARM2C
LTJG. JOHN R. LINDBECK
JOHN A. LINSON, ARM1C
JEROME R. MAGEE, ARM3C
JAMES W. MASSEY, PHOM3C
LTJG. EDWARD L. MATHIAS
ENS. RALPH D. MCAFEE
WILLIAM D. MC DONNELL, ARM2C
LTJG. GORDON E. MC GLOTHLIN
ENS. ROBERT W. O'CALLAHAN
LTJG. BERT H. PARKS

ZIEGLER F. PIERCEFIELD, PTR3C
EDWARD A. PORTER, ARM2C
LTJG. PAUL H. PRANDINI
LTJG. BRYANT E. PRICHARD
LTJG. WILLIAM W. REITER
LTJG. JOHN M. ROBINSON, JR.
ENS. WILLIAM J. SEYFFERLE
LTJF. JAMES A. SHIELDS, JR
HOMER L. SIKES, ARM3C
ROBERT SPALDING, ARM2C
LTJG. ARTHUR H. SPARROW
ENS. ARTHUR W. SPINDLER
WILLIAM W. STEVENS, AMM2C
ELVIN W. STOUFFER, ARM2C
LTJG. JOHN W. THOMPSON
JOHN W. TURNER, AMM3C
DONALD F. TUSSING, AOM3C
FRANK E. VANDEVENTER, AMM3C
LTJG. NORMAN E. WHITE

AIR GROUP 19

EDWARD R. ALBINI, ARM2
LT. COMDR. DONALD F. BANKER
LTJG. CLARENCE E. BARTLETT
LTJG. ROBERT W. BLAKESLEE
MICHAEL K. BLAZEVICH, ARM1C
LT. ROGER S. BOLES
FRED R. BURKHARDT, CPHOMA
LT. HOWARD R. BURNETT
JAMES J. BURNS, ARM2C
FRANK J. CAKA, JR. ARM2C
LTJG. JOHN A. CAVANAUGH, JR.
LT. COMDR. FRANKLIN E. COOK
LAMARK DEES, AOM2C
ENS. DAN G. DELUCA, JR.
ENS. ROBERT W. DOYLE
LTJG. JOHN W. EVATT
WILLIAM W. FINGER, ARM1C

LTJG. CHARLES F. FISHER
ENS. PAUL A. GEVELINGER
ENS. JOHN W. GILCHRIST
LTJG. ROBERT H.H. GOFORTH
ENS. ALTON W. HALLOWELL
RICHARD W. HANSEN, ARM3C
ENS. FRANCIS P. HUBBUCH
ENS. FRANCIS O. JACKSON
ORVILLE F. JASPER, ARM2C
JOHN JOHNSTON, ARM1C
LTJG. JOSEPH KELLY
PHILLIP D. LARGO, ARM3C
WILLIAM C. LYDE, ARM3C
ENS. ROY F. MAJORS
ENS. WILLIAM H. MARTIN
WILLIAM L. MARTIN, ARM2C
ENS. ROBERT K. MC ADAMS

COMDR. RICHARD MC GOWAN
LTJG. JOHN MIDDLETON, JR
JACK C. MITCHELL, AOM2C
LTJG. JOHN M. MORRISON
BERNARD F. MURPHY, ARM2C
LOUIS O. NITCHMAN, ARM3C
LT. ROBERT B. PARKER
JAMES C. REESE, AOM2C
ENS. ALFRED N. RUFFCORN
LTJG. ROBERT L. SINCLAIR
LTJG. ROBERT O. SMITH
JOHN R. SNOW, JR. ARM2C
ENS. WILLIAM E. STRUNK
LT. DONALD K. TRIPP
ENS. BLAIR M. WAKEFIELD
LTJG. CHARLES E. WENDT

AIR GROUP 20

HARRY J. ALDRO, ARM2C
ENS. MARVEL D. ALLEN
LTJG. DOUGLAS BAKER
LTJG. JAMES W. BECKMAN
JOHN F. BRADY, JR. ARM3C
LTJG. PHILLIPS J. BRADLEY
ENS. HOYT A. CARLTON
LTJG. JAMES G. DARRACOTT
ROBERT W. DYKES, ARM1C
CHESTER O. EVANS, ARM2C
CLIFFORD B. GALLANT, AMM3C
ENS. GLEN E. GORDON

LT. HERBERT C. HOGAN
LTJG. DAVID F. HUGHES
LTJG. HERBERT A. KOSTER
LT. MARTIN L. LEEDOM
EUGENE G. LONG, ACRMA
WILLIAM E. MC GRATH, ARM1
ENS. GEORGE W. MC JINSEY
CHARLES E. MC VAY, AOM2C
BURNAL L. MURR, ARM3C
ENS. GAYLORD W. NEAL
LT. JOHN E. NEARING

LTJG. ROBERT D. OLSON
GORDON E. RICKEILL, AOM2C
ENS. JAMES W. ROBINSON
LTJG. DAN J. RYAN JR.
WILLIAM J. SCHNEIDER, AMM2C
LTJG. DONALD F. SEIZ
LTJG. DONALD D. J. SPANAGEL
W. R. TEMPLETON, ARM4
LTJG. JOHN E. TSARNAS
DEWEY C. WARREN ARM2C
CLARENCE W. WATERS, ARM2C
LT. RUSSELL S. WILCOX

AIR GROUP 9

LT. WILLIAM M. HILKENS
LTJG. WALTER A. JACOBS, JR.
THEO S. MALIKOWSKI, AQM1C

LTJG. ROBERT L. PARKER
CHARLES B. ROSSI, ARM1C

ENS. WALTER J. SCHMISSEUR
COMDR. PHILIP H. TORREY, JR.
ENS. FLOYD E. TURNER

AIR GROUP 94

LTJG. MILTON L. ADAMS
LT. LAWSON J. BAULIES
MELFORD W. HENDRIKSON, ARM2C
ENS. LEWIS F. PETTIS, JR.
LT. RALPH BOROS
LTJG. THOMAS BRETT

LTJG. EDWARD CLANCY
ENS. ROBERT T. CUNNINGHAM
LTJG. BARHAM F. DILLARD, JR.
ENS. EDWARD W. GARRISON
CLARENCE M. GRAY, ARMSC
ENS. ALFRED L. MORRIS
LTJG. JOHN E. O'NEIL, JR.

LT. NICHOLAS M. PAVONETTI
ENS. MERLE E. L. PENNINGTON
LTJG. NEWHY H. POPE
ENS. NORTON E. SIMS
LTJG. CLIFFORD W. SNYDER
ENS. FRANCIS M. TAYLOR

IN FOND MEMORY OF OUR DEAR DEPARTED SHIPMATES WHO GAVE THEIR LIVES TO GOD AND THEIR COUNTRY DURING WORLD WAR II IN ORDER TO PRESERVE OUR RIGHTS TO REMAIN A FREE AND INDEPENDENT NATION. DONATED BY THE U.S.S. LEXINGTON CV-16 ASSOCIATION.

This book is dedicated to all of the Americans who gave their lives aboard the USS LEXINGTON during World War II. Their names are listed on this plaque which is located in the hangar bay of the ship. Included are names of the ship's company, and Air Groups 16, 19, 20, 9, and 94.

THE ESSEX CLASS OF WORLD WAR II

Taken on June 14, 1944, this photograph shows the LEXINGTON as she supported the landings in the Marianas. The flight deck markings have become considerably worn and are almost impossible to see. Rub marks made by the arresting cables on the aft end of the flight deck are visible. (National Archives)

The following table provides basic chronological information on each of the ESSEX class carriers prior to their post-war modernizations.

NUMBER AND NAME	BUILDER	KEEL LAID	LAUNCHED	COMMISSIONED	DECOMMISSIONED
CV-9 ESSEX (SH)	NNSDDC	4/28/41	7/31/42	12/31/42	1/9/47
CV-10 YORKTOWN (SH)	NNSDDC	1/1/41	1/21/43	4/15/43	1/9/47
CV-11 INTREPID (SH)	NNSDDC	12/1/41	4/26/43	8/16/43	3/22/47
CV-12 HORNET (SH)	NNSDDC	8/3/42	8/30/43	11/29/43	1/15/47
CV-13 FRANKLIN (SH)	NNSDDC	12/7/42	10/14/43	1/31/44	2/17/47
CV-14 TICONDEROGA	NNSDDC	2/1/43	2/7/44	5/8/44	1/9/47
CV-15 RANDOLPH	NNSDDC	5/10/43	6/29/44	10/9/44	6/47
CV-16 LEXINGTON (SH)	**BSQM**	**9/15/41**	**9/26/42**	**2/17/43**	**4/23/47**
CV-17 BUNKER HILL (SH)	BSQM	9/15/41	12/7/42	5/25/43	1/47
CV-18 WASP (SH)	BSQM	3/18/42	8/17/43	11/24/43	2/17/47
CV-19 HANCOCK	BSQM	1/26/43	8/17/43	4/15/44	5/9/47
CV-20 BENNINGTON (SH)	NNSDDC	12/15/42	2/26/44	8/6/44	11/8/46
CV-21 BOXER	NNSDDC	9/13/43	12/14/44	4/16/45	12/1/69
CV-31 BON HOMME RICHARD (SH)	NYNY	2/1/43	4/29/44	11/26/44	1/9/47
CV-32 LEYTE	NNSDDC	2/21/44	8/23/45	4/11/46	5/15/59
CV-33 KEARSARGE	NYNY	3/1/44	5/5/45	3/2/46	6/16/50
CV-34 ORISKANY	NYNY	5/1/44	10/13/45	9/25/50	5/15/76
CV-35 REPRISAL	NYNY	7/1/44	CONSTRUCTION CANCELLED		8/12/45
CV-36 ANTIETAM	PNY	3/15/43	8/20/44	1/28/45	6/21/49
CV-37 PRINCETON	PNY	9/14/43	7/8/45	11/18/45	6/21/49
CV-38 SHANGRI-LA	NNY	1/15/43	2/24/44	9/15/44	11/7/47
CV-39 LAKE CHAMPLAIN	NNY	3/15/43	11/2/44	6/3/45	3/46
CV-40 TARAWA	NNY	3/1/44	5/12/45	12/8/45	6/30/49
CV-45 VALLEY FORGE	PNY	9/7/44	11/18/45	11/3/46	1/15/70
CV-46 IWO JIMA	PNY	1/29/45	CONSTRUCTION CANCELLED		8/12/45
CV-47 PHILIPPINE SEA	BSQM	8/19/44	9/5/45	5/11/46	12/58

BUILDERS:
- NNSDDC — NEWPORT NEWS SHIPBUILDING AND DRY DOCK COMPANY
- BSQM — BETHLEHEM STEEL, QUINCY, MASSACHUSETTS
- NYNY — NEW YORK NAVY YARD
- PNY — PHILADELPHIA NAVY YARD
- NNY — NORFOLK NAVY YARD

(SH) INDICATES A SHORT HULL SHIP. ALL OTHERS ARE LONG HULL SHIPS.

WORLD WAR II HISTORY

The date is February 17, 1943, the place is Boston Harbor, the weather is very cold, as evidenced by the ice in the water and the snow on the flight deck, and CV-16 has just been commissioned the USS LEXINGTON. This photograph shows a number of the ship's details as completed. Note that there is only one catapult. The port catapult was not installed at this time. There are five lattice radio masts along the starboard side of the flight deck. As a short hull unit of the ESSEX class, there was only one 40mm gun mount on the bow. There is little in the way of radar antennas on the superstructure. The forward elevator is lowered, and the port deck edge elevator is folded to the vertical position. Being commissioned on February 17, 1943, (not March 17, as stated in some other publications) LEXINGTON was the second ESSEX class carrier to enter service with the U.S. Navy. The ESSEX was commissioned on December 31, 1942.

(National Archives)

The USS LEXINGTON, CV-16, was built at the Fore River Shipyard at Quincy, Massachusetts, and was commissioned at the South Boston Navy Yard on February 17, 1943. Captain F. B. Stump, USN, became the first commanding officer. She had originally been named USS CABOT, but the name was changed to LEXINGTON, when the first carrier to bear that name, CV-2, was lost at the Battle of Coral Sea on May 8, 1942. This began a precedent, as each fleet carrier that was lost during the war had a new carrier under construction named for it. These included YORKTOWN, WASP, HORNET, and PRINCETON. Even the old LANGLEY, CV-1, which had been converted to a seaplane tender, AV-3, had a carrier named for it when it was sunk on February 27, 1942. In this case, the new carrier was CVL-27, a light carrier of the INDEPENDENCE class, but for all of the other carriers that were lost, it was a new ESSEX class carrier that carried on the name of the ship that was lost.

The name originally planned for these ships was then used for a subsequent carrier. The name CABOT must have been a blessing for longevity of service. It was originally to be the name of CV-16, which still remains in service with the U.S. Navy. When this ship was renamed LEXINGTON, the name CABOT was given to CVL-28, which went to war carrying that name. After post-war service with the U.S. Navy, and a redesignation to AVT-3, she was transferred to Spain in 1967, and renamed DEDALO. Thus she became the last of the INDEPENDENCE class light carriers to remain in service.

The name LEXINGTON is one of the most famous in U.S. Navy history. The first LEXINGTON was a sixteen-gun brig that was purchased in March 1776 by the Continental Congress. The second LEXINGTON was a 691-ton sloop that was commissioned on June 11, 1826. She saw service in the Mexican War, and later was a storeship for Commodore Perry's expedition to Japan. She was followed by the third LEXINGTON which was an ironclad sidewheeler that was commissioned in August of 1861. After seeing action in the Civil War, she was decommissioned on June 2, 1865. The next LEXINGTON was to be a battlecruiser, but became the U.S. Navy's second aircraft carrier CV-2. She was commissioned on December 14, 1927, and as mentioned earlier, was lost at the Battle of Coral Sea.

Detail of the two portside screws and shafts are seen in this photograph of the LEXINGTON while she was still on the building ways at Quincy, Massachusetts.
(National Archives)

CDR B. W. Wright is catapulted from the LEXINGTON in an F4F Wildcat to record the first take off from the new carrier. The top of the catapult bridle can be seen at the very bottom of the photograph. CDR Wright had made the first of what would someday exceed 500,000 arrested landings just before this photograph was taken on April 23, 1943.
(National Archives)

The present LEXINGTON was the second ESSEX class carrier to be commissioned. After her commissioning, LEXINGTON began a fitting out period at Boston, then she left for the Chesapeake Bay on April 13th. On April 23rd, CDR B.W. Wright made the first take-off and landing aboard the ship. She was then joined by Air Group 16 for practice maneuvers. After a shakedown cruise, she returned to Boston for post shakedown availability.

Following her post shakedown availability, LEXINGTON left Boston and proceeded via Norfolk to the Panama Canal. On July 26th, she joined with the BELLEAU WOOD, CVL-24, and PRINCETON, CVL-23, and transited the Canal on July 26th and 27th. On July 28th, these three carriers, along with the other ships of Task Group 52.6 left Balboa and headed for Pearl Harbor. After an uneventful voyage, LEXINGTON arrived at Pearl Harbor on August 9th, and reported to ComAirPac for duty as part of the Pacific Fleet.

After several weeks at Pearl Harbor, LEXINGTON left for war on September 11th, as part of CTG 15.5. The mission of this group was to make a raid on enemy air installations at Tarawa Atoll in the Gilbert Islands. The raid began at dawn on September 18th, and during that day 196 sorties were flown with a loss of only three aircraft. After the raid, the group returned to Pearl Harbor.

LEXINGTON sortied on September 29th for her second raid which was a strike against Wake Island. This was to be the first raid carried out by several carrier groups operating together. In two days Air Group 16 flew 305 sorties with the loss of two fighters and one dive bomber. The bomber crew was rescued by a submarine.

The next operation for LEXINGTON was the occupa-

Air Group 16 operated on the LEXINGTON during her shakedown cruise. At that time the F4F Wildcat had not been replaced by the F6F Hellcat, but it was the only time the Wildcat would operate from this carrier. By the time LEXINGTON left for the Pacific on July 4, 1943, Air Group 16 had received the Hellcat. This F4F has missed the arresting cables and is about to hit the barriers. Details of the superstructure are visible in this photograph.
(National Archives)

*The first F6F-3 Hellcat to land aboard the LEXINGTON comes aboard on July 5, 1943, as Air Group 16 joins the carrier en route to the Pacific via the Panama Canal. At this time the number **16** was not visible on the flight deck.*
(National Archives)

9

1943

This view is similar to the commissioning photograph shown at the top of page 8. The photograph was taken on May 28, 1943, just over three months after the commissioning, and noteworthy is the addition of radar and other antennas to the superstructure. The lattice masts are lowered to the horizontal position as they would be for flight operations. There is a noticeable weathering of paint visible along the sides of the ship. (National Archives)

Also taken on May 28, 1943, during LEXINGTON's shakedown cruise, this photograph reveals details on the port side. Note that there is only one 40mm gun mount located to the left of the centerline on the stern. The four five-inch single gun mounts can be seen on this side of the carrier. Two are located forward, and two aft. (National Archives)

*This excellent view of the LEXINGTON was taken on October 10, 1943, shortly after the raids on Wake Island. The number **16** now appears on the flight deck.* (National Archives)

F6F-3s and SBDs are shown preparing for take-off for the raids on Mille Island in November 1943.
(National Archives)

*Returning aircraft from the Mille raids are parked forward. Note that the Hellcat that is taxiing forward has the red surround on the national insignia. At this time the Air Group had no distinguishing markings on its aircraft. A part of the **16** on the forward end of the flight deck is visible in this photograph.* *(National Archives)*

tion of the Gilbert Islands during November 19th-24th. Working with YORKTOWN, CV-10, and COWPENS, CVL-25, LEXINGTON took up a station 100 miles southeast of Mille in the Marshalls group. Their mission was to intercept enemy aircraft being staged from the Marshalls to counter the invasion of the Gilberts. They also conducted strikes against installations at Mille. On November 23rd, twelve Hellcats from LEXINGTON shot down seventeen Japanese aircraft and claimed an additional three probables. Only one Hellcat was lost, and its pilot was rescued. The next day, twelve Hellcats attacked a formation of two Bettys and eighteen Zekes. They shot down both Bettys and ten Zekes with two more as probables. No Hellcats were lost.

After refueling, the carrier groups proceeded on to raid Kwajalein Atoll. The first strike was made at 0630 on the morning of December 4th. Dive and torpedo bombers attacked the two cruisers and a transport in the harbor, destroying the transport and damaging the cruisers. Twelve Hellcats strafed the airfield, although they were intercepted by thirty Japanese fighters from Roi Island. Nineteen enemy fighters and one Betty were destroyed in the air, and three more Bettys were destroyed on the ground. While returning from the strike, the SBDs were attacked by enemy fighters. The SBDs shot down six Zekes and one Betty on their way back to the ship. The final score for Air Group 16 for this strike was one transport and one cruiser sunk, one cruiser damaged, 27 aircraft shot down, and three destroyed on the ground.

As the group withdrew, they were attacked by two enemy torpedo bombers. The gunners on the LEXINGTON were the first to open fire in what was to be their first chance to engage in actual combat. They shot down both aircraft in quick order. Then a third bomber was sighted. It dropped its torpedo, but was then shot down by LEXINGTON gunners. An evasive turn caused the torpedo to

The list on the flight deck is noticeable in this photograph as the LEXINGTON makes a hard turn to starboard. Hellcats with folded wings and Dauntless dive bombers are on the deck. *(National Archives)*

The ship's only catapult is being used to launch SBDs in late November 1943. Note the wind sock on the side of the twin five-inch mount, and the forward-most barrier stretching across the deck in the down position. These SBDs were probably being launched for patrol duty rather than for a raid when this photograph was taken.
(National Archives)

This view, taken in brighter light, shows more details of the LEXINGTON on November 12, 1943. Note the two new 40mm gun positions at the hangar deck level on the aft end of the ship. These were not present at her commissioning nor during the shakedown cruise.
(National Archives)

miss.

That evening, at 1846, radar detected the first bogie, then more and more were seen. From then until 0127, the Task Group was under continual attack. At 2150, float lights were dropped on the water to guide the attackers to the target. At 2322, four parachute flares appeared on the port beam of the LEXINGTON silhouetting the ship, and making it obvious that it had been picked out as a target. At 2325, LEXINGTON opened fire at bogies coming in from the starboard bow. A torpedo was seen to drop from a Betty on the starboard beam, and the torpedo hit at 2332. The damage caused the ship to settle five feet to starboard, and steering control was lost. The carrier turned in a circle to port streaming a dense cloud of smoke from ruptured gas tanks on the fantail. Nine men died and thirty-two were wounded in the attack.

After twenty minutes, the rudder was brought amidships, and steering was accomplished by using the main engine. Only half an hour after being hit, LEXINGTON was steaming eastward at 20 knots. It continued on to Pearl Harbor for temporary repairs, then on to Bremerton for permanent repairs, arriving there on December 22nd in time for Christmas.

LEXINGTON left Bremerton on February 20th, and proceeded to NAS Alameda to pick up Air Group 19, 2500 passengers, and freight. She passed under the Golden Gate Bridge on February 24th, and arrived at Pearl Harbor on February 28th. With her old Air Group 16 back aboard, LEXINGTON left for the war zone on March 3rd. She arrived at Majuro in the Marshalls on March 8th, where Vice Admiral Marc A. Mitscher moved his flag aboard, thus making LEXINGTON the Force Flagship of Task Force 58.

On March 18, LEXINGTON and Air Group 16 conducted their first strikes since being damaged in December. The target was Mille Atoll which was still in Japanese hands. Two days later, the Task Force headed for their next major operation, a raid on the Palau Islands. On March 29th, from 1712 to 2200, the Task Force was subjected to a night attack, but no damage was done, and the ship secured from General Quarters. At 0633 the next morning, the first strikes were launched, and they continued uninterrupted throughout the rest of that day and the next. The next day strikes were launched against Woleai, putting it permanently out of action as a Japanese staging base. The Task Force then returned to Majuro Atoll, arriving there on April 16th. While there, Captain Stump was promoted to Rear Admiral, and Captain E. N. Litch replaced him as commanding officer of the LEXINGTON on April 10th.

Task Force 58 then sailed for Hollandia, New Guinea, to support landings by the Army. Strikes commenced on April 21st, with 212 sorties being flown that day. Twenty-nine enemy aircraft were destroyed on the ground, and two costal vessels were sunk. The following day the landings were conducted against minimal opposition, and only 74 sorties were flown.

While the operation against Hollandia was relatively

This plaque is located on the starboard side of the fantail at the hangar deck level, just above where an aerial torpedo struck the ship on December 4, 1943. It was the first damage inflicted on the LEXINGTON by the Japanese.

With only two aircraft on the flight deck, this excellent overhead view shows the flight deck markings on the LEXINGTON very well. The markings were black on a blue stained deck. This photograph was taken on March 10, 1944, just two days after Vice Admiral Marc Mitscher moved his flag aboard the ship. (National Archives)

easy, the next operation was against Truk, which had the reputation of being Japan's strongest base in the Pacific. The run-in during the evening of April 28th was uneventful, and launching of the first strikes the following morning was delayed until 0722 due to bad weather. Shortly after 0800, bogies were reported, and at 0814 two dive bombers made runs against LEXINGTON from the port bow. One was shot down, and the other one dropped a bomb which fell just off the fantail.

Meanwhile, the first strike reached the target area, and was intercepted by many Japanese fighters. Hellcats from the LEXINGTON shot down seventeen with a loss of four planes and three pilots. Fighters from the LANGLEY, CVL-27, shot down another twenty fighters. From then on, enemy air resistance was negligible, and for two days Task Force 58 systematically worked over Truk, while cruisers and battleships pounded the neighboring islands of Satawan and Ponape. At times the force was so close to the outlying islands that they could be seen on the horizon. An enemy dive bomber dropped a bomb close to the LEXINGTON during the second evening of the attack, but otherwise there was no further enemy activity over the ships.

The force returned to Majuro for replenishment, then departed on June 6th, for the Marianas. On the afternoon of June 11th, a fighter sweep was launched at 1307. Task Force fighters shot down over 100 enemy aircraft during the sweep, and effectively neutralized air opposition over Saipan. The enemy launched numerous attacks against the Task Force, but no damage was done except for loss of a lot of sleep. On June 12th, the LEXINGTON launched a fighter sweep at dawn, and this was followed by six strikes against Saipan. Severe damage was inflicted on ground installations, and two cargo ships and several smaller craft were sunk by LEXINGTON's aircraft. A fighter sweep and four strikes were launched the following day. Although these were successful, the day was marred by the loss of CDR Robert Isley, the commanding officer of the torpedo squadron. He was hit by AA fire, and crashed on the airfield that was later named in his honor.

On June 14th, more strikes were conducted on the northern islands and on Saipan itself. Strikes continued the following day. At 1803, while still in the process of landing planes from the last strike, a bogie was picked up on radar and shot down by CAP from one of the other carriers. At 1818, General Quarters was sounded while landing operations continued. The Japanese attack was large and executed at very high speed. LEXINGTON's gun batteries shot down five of eight enemy aircraft that appeared off her starboard and port bows. Two torpedoes were launched at the ship, and one passed on each side as the ship maneuvered. They were very close and in plain view of the crewmen on the deck. One attacker burst into flames on the port bow, then flew the length of the flight deck only a few feet above it. The aircraft crashed off the port quarter, but there were no serious injuries sustained by any of the LEXINGTON's crew.

Not much happened until June 19th, which became famous as the date of the first Battle of the Philippine Sea. During the day, the LEXINGTON's air group did its full share. While the dive and torpedo bombers were hitting Guam, the fighters shot down forty-five aircraft that attacked the task force. The CAP from all of the carriers

1944

After receiving a torpedo hit in the stern on December 4, 1943, LEXINGTON returned to Puget Sound for repairs and other work. The photographs on this page were all taken on February 20, 1944, as the ship left Puget Sound heading for San Francisco. Two changes in particular are noteworthy. First, the second catapult has been added to the port side. Second, three 40mm gun sponsons have been added to the starboard side just below the island. LEXINGTON was one of the first-if not the first-ESSEX class carrier to receive these extra gun mounts. There remains only one 40mm mount on the bow and one on the stern.

(All photos, National Archives)

This view of the port side shows more 40mm gun mounts that were added at Puget Sound. Two quad 40mm tubs have been located at the hangar deck level forward of the deck edge elevator and aft of the forward five-inch guns. In this photograph, the carrier is recovering aircraft from strikes on Palau in late March 1944. (National Archives)

Details of the starboard side of the ship are visible in this photograph taken in March 1944. (National Archives)

Front and rear views of the LEXINGTON show additional details of the ship as she operates off Palau in March 1944. In the photograph at left, notice the Hellcat at the extreme right that has taken a wave-off and is flying along the side of the ship. (Both National Archives)

15

proved more than a match for the enemy, and gun batteries from the ships took care of the few enemy planes that did get through. Fighters landed, rearmed, and refueled, then launched again to maintain the protective umbrella above the ships. By the end of the day, over 400 enemy aircraft had been destroyed.

The next day was spent searching for Japanese surface units, and twelve Hellcats armed with bombs were launched from LEXINGTON. They searched out to 450 miles, but made no contact. They returned after a search mission lasting six hours. But at 1545, a search plane from one of the other Task Groups in the force located the enemy. In spite of the lateness of the hour and the great distance involved, a strike was prepared. LEXINGTON launched eleven Hellcats, seven Avengers, and fifteen Dauntless dive bombers at 1635.

It was dark when the aircraft from the strike began returning to the force. They were running low on gas, and it was feared that many might have to ditch at sea in the darkness. They were landed aboard the first carrier they found even if it was not their assigned carrier. It was at this time that Vice Admiral Mitscher on the LEXINGTON gave the famous order to "Turn on the lights," violating light security in order to help the returning pilots find their way home. It risked exposing the force to an enemy submarine or aircraft, but the order now is among the most famous given in the history of the U.S. Navy, and ranks with, "I have not yet begun to fight," and "Damn the torpedoes, full speed ahead." Fortunately, no enemy attack was made, and many planes landed safely while others ditched close to the ships.

For the balance of this operation, which lasted until July 9th, "milk run" strikes were made against Guam to deny its use to the enemy. At 0630 on July 9th, Air Group 16 launched for the last time. This was also the last time that the SBD Dauntless would launch from the LEXINGTON. Other carriers had already changed to the SB2C Helldiver, and LEXINGTON was now to do so as well. Even as Air Group 16 left, planes from Air Group 19 were seen overhead, and all were safely aboard by 0846.

On July 14th, LEXINGTON sortied from Eniwetok, and once again headed for the Marianas. From July 18th to 21st, they supported the landings on Guam. On July 24th, they conducted strikes against Palau, Yap, and Ulithi. Throughout this period air opposition was nonexistent, and activities were conducted in a routine manner. On the afternoon of July 21st, LEXINGTON was again in the Marianas, and anchored in Saipan harbor. Here the ship was replenished, and then she left to conduct strikes on Iwo Jima, Haha Jima, and Chiohi Jima. She then returned to Eniwetok on August 10th and remained there until August 29th.

On September 6th, 7th, and 8th, the task group conducted strikes on Palau with no airborne opposition. This ended the assaults on the outlying islands, and from this point on, the attention of the Third Fleet was turned to the Philippines and the inner circle of Japan's defenses. On

One of the most famous orders in naval history was given by Vice Admiral Marc Mitscher during the First Battle of the Philippine Sea on June 20, 1944. To help returning aircraft to find the ships, Admiral Mitscher ordered the ships to "Turn on the lights," thus possibly exposing them to enemy aircraft and submarines. The gamble paid off, and this plaque now commemorates the order that was given aboard the USS LEXINGTON.

September 9th and 10th, Mindanao was hit by strikes from the entire task force. Then, looking for targets, Admiral Halsey ordered strikes against the Visayan region. Here, the fighters found the opposition they had been looking for. On September 12th, a fighter sweep ran into planes taking off from airfields in the Cebu area, and shot down fifteen enemy aircraft. On September 21st and 22nd, strikes were begun in the Manila area.

After replenishment at Ulithi, LEXINGTON participated in strikes against Okinawa on October 10th, and on Formosa from October 12th through the 14th. The first fighter sweep encountered many enemy planes, and shot down twenty-eight of them. The ships of the task force were not attacked during the day, but came under sustained attack at night. On the second evening, the cruiser CANBERRA took a torpedo hit, so instead of retiring, the force stayed on to assist her and to make further diversionary attacks on Formosa. The following afternoon, the force was again attacked. A torpedo narrowly missed the ESSEX, and a Japanese plane crash-dived into the fantail of the cruiser RENO, causing minor damage. The CAP from the PRINCETON shot down eighteen planes of the attacking force.

On October 24, the task group began strikes against Luzon, while the rest of the task force was operating to the south. At 0800, radar plot reported "many many" bogies closing, and all available fighters were scrambled.

The force was under constant attack throughout the day from carrier and shore-based aircraft, but the effective CAP adequately protected the ships. Only a few isolated enemy planes got through, and one of those dropped a bomb on PRINCETON. This caused secondary explosions of armed aircraft on her hangar deck, and despite a gallant effort, she was eventually lost. She was the only CV or CVL lost after the first HORNET, CV-8, was sunk at the Battle of Santa Cruz on October 26, 1942. One hundred and fifty enemy planes were shot down by the task group.

On the morning of October 25th, strikes were launched against an enemy carrier force to the north. This was one of the more controversial decisions made during the war in the Pacific. Admiral Halsey decided to hit Admiral Ozawa's carriers to deal the few remaining carrier forces of Japan a decisive blow. It was Ozawa's mission to act as a decoy and draw Halsey north to attack the Japanese carriers that were now lacking any kind of credible force of aircraft. The correctness of the decision will not be debated here. Halsey wanted to crush the last of the Japanese carrier forces, and this he did. Only twenty Zeke fighters rose to intercept the American aircraft, and these were easily smothered by the Hellcats. This allowed the bombers to work slowly and deliberately, and strike after strike was thrown at the enemy throughout the day. The carriers CHITOSE, CHIYODA, ZUIHO, and ZUIKAKU were sunk. The enemy force was crushed, and for all intents and purposes, Japanese carrier forces ceased to exist. After this battle, known as the Second Battle of the Philippine Sea, Vice Admiral Mitscher and his staff departed the LEXINGTON.

Following a replenishment period, two strikes were begun off Luzon on November 5th and 6th. Aircraft struck the Clark Field area, and LEXINGTON's planes sunk a heavy cruiser in Manila Bay. But the Japanese were to retaliate. At 1315, bogies were reported, and when they approached to ten miles without being intercepted, it was obvious that LEXINGTON was to come under attack. At 1337, two Zekes dived on the ship. A five-inch shell knocked off the tail of the first, causing it to miss the ship, but the second, although hit, continued on into the ship, crashing just aft of the secondary conn. Heavy fires ensued, and numerous casualties were suffered. The fires were quickly controlled, and with the flight deck undamaged, air operations continued. Forty-seven men were killed and 127 were wounded. After conducting strikes the following day, LEXINGTON retired to Ulithi where the wounded were transferred to the USS SOLACE.

For the rest of November, LEXINGTON underwent repairs. Air Group 19 returned to the States, and was replaced with Air Group 20 from ENTERPRISE. They brought seventy-three Hellcats, fifteen Avengers, and fifteen Helldivers with them. On December 11th, LEXINGTON sortied from Ulithi as flagship of CTG 58.2, to support the landings of General MacArthur's forces at Mindoro. Strikes were made on December 14th, 15th, and 16th to blanket the airfields and prevent air opposition of the landings. This effort was so successful that no enemy opposition was encountered during this period. On the morning of the 16th, a small group of Bettys and Zekes was detected heading toward the force, but these were intercepted by fighters from LEXINGTON and HANCOCK, CV-19, and all enemy aircraft were shot down. On December 23, the force returned to Ulithi after riding out a typhoon.

LEXINGTON again sortied from Ulithi on December 30th, and until her return on January 27, she participated in strikes against Formosa, Luzon, Camranh Bay, Hong Kong, and Okinawa. After her return to Ulithi, Captain Litch was relieved by Captain Thomas H. Robbins as the ship's commanding officer. The following day, Rear

Single and twin barrel 20mm guns formed the close-in anti-aircraft defense for the LEXINGTON. Dozens of these guns lined the flight deck. They put up a lot of fire, and could discourage even the bravest pilot, but had little effect against a Kamikaze. The only way to stop a suicide dive was to blow the aircraft apart before it hit the ship.
(National Archives)

Medium range defense was supplied by quad 40mm mounts. These were located on the hangar deck level, the flight deck level, and on the superstructure.
(National Archives)

SUICIDE DIVE

Careful examination of this photograph will reveal a speck above the USS LEXINGTON that is in reality a Japanese Zeke making a suicide dive on the ship. White puffs of smoke indicate the intensity of the anti-aircraft fire. The photograph was taken only seconds before impact. (National Archives)

This dramatic photograph was taken looking almost straight up at the Zeke making its suicide dive on the ship. Tracers can be seen heading for the aircraft, and although hit, the pilot managed to guide the Zeke into the secondary conn of the ship. (National Archives)

Impact! This enlarged photo shows the smoke and fire resulting from the suicide aircraft hitting the superstructure. Since the flight deck was undamaged, the carrier was able to resume flight operations in a short time, but then headed to Ulithi for repairs the next day. (National Archives)

These two photographs show part of the damage caused by the suicide attack. Most of the casualties were in the exposed 20mm gun batteries. (Both National Archives)

This is the plot room of the USS LEXINGTON as it appeared in January 1945. (National Archives)

Air Group 20 was aboard the LEXINGTON when this photograph was taken at Ulithi in February 1945. Notice that the Hellcats are the F6F-5 version, and are in overall gloss sea blue. The Helldivers and Avengers are still in the three-color scheme. All have the LEXINGTON's markings for that time, consisting of a large diagonal white band on the vertical tail and the upper surfaces of the wings. (National Archives)

Admiral R. E. Davidson of Carrier Division 2 raised his flag aboard LEXINGTON. Air Group 9 replaced Air Group 20 on February 2. This new group got its baptism of fire in strikes around Tokyo on February 16 and 17. On the 16th, twenty-five enemy planes were shot down, and eighteen more were destroyed on the ground. The Air Group Commander, CDR P. H. Torrey, Jr., and three other pilots were lost during the day. Three Zekes and an Oscar were shot down the following day, which was the second anniversary of the commissioning of the LEXINGTON.

The strikes in the Tokyo area were followed by more strikes in support of the landings on Iwo Jima on February 19th, 21st, and 22nd. On the 25th, the group returned for another strike around Tokyo. After a strike and photo mission at Amami Gunto on March 1, the LEXINGTON returned to Ulithi. On March 7th, the LEXINGTON left Ulithi for a trip back to the States. After stopping at Pearl Harbor, she entered Puget Sound Navy Yard and Bremerton, Washington, on March 31.

LEXINGTON remained all of April and part of May at Puget Sound. Most work was simply a routine overhaul, but a noteworthy change to the superstructure was made. The flag plot and navigation bridge was enlarged, and this necessitated the removal of the forward most 40mm gun mount on the superstructure. The other noticeable

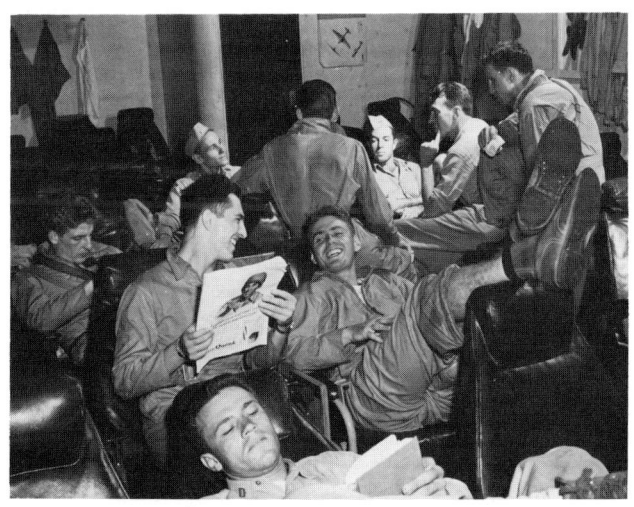

Pilots relax in one of the ship's ready rooms. Note the aircraft silhouette photograph on the wall to the rear of the room. (National Archives)

Other officers are shown relaxing in the flight deck control office in December 1944. More interesting silhouette photographs appear on these walls!

(National Archives)

Ferrying a lot of passengers and land-based aircraft, the LEXINGTON leaves NAS Alameda on May 29, 1945. The graded Measure 12 paint scheme is visible, consisting of the darker Navy Blue or Navy Gray from the waterline up to the hangar deck, and Ocean Gray from the hangar deck up. Many references have previously reported this as Measure 22, with Navy Blue up to the hangar deck and Haze Gray from there on up. Recent studies have indicated that it was Measure 12 instead. The darker, lower color could have been Navy Blue, or, more probably, Navy Gray, but black and white photographs do not verify this. The flight deck is stained blue. Noteworthy is the additional 40mm quad mount on the fantail. Only the forward two lattice radio masts remain. The masts aft of the superstructure have been removed. (National Archives)

change was that the LEXINGTON was no longer painted in the overall Sea Blue of Measure 21. Instead, she had been repainted in Measure 22, a graded system of Navy Gray or Navy Blue up to the hangar deck level, and Ocean Gray from there on up. LEXINGTON left Bremerton on May 22nd, and headed for NAS Alameda, California. On May 29th, she left for Pearl Harbor without escort.

At Pearl Harbor, Air Group 94 came on board. This group was the first to bring the F4U Corsair aboard LEXINGTON. The group had 103 aircraft, consisting of thirty-one Hellcat fighters, four Hellcat night fighters, two photographic Hellcats, thirty-six Corsairs, fifteen Hell-

The LEXINGTON was about ready to leave the Puget Sound Navy Yard on May 14, 1945, when this photograph of the superstructure was taken. Note the Bugs Bunny character on the forward director. (National Archives)

This photograph shows details of the superstructure on May 23, 1945, as the ship sailed toward NAS Alameda from Puget Sound. Note the lowered forward elevator and radar fit. Of particular interest is the removal of the forward-most 40mm quad mount from the superstructure and the enlarged flag plot and navigation bridge in its former location. (National Archives)

Late in the war, the LEXINGTON became the only ESSEX class carrier fitted with Army quad .50 caliber machine gun mounts that were used for close-in air defense. Confidence was not high with the 20mm guns when it came to knocking down a Kamikaze, and the quad fifties could put out more firepower. Seven such mounts were installed. The one shown at left is on the port side, and the one at right is on the starboard side. (Both National Archives)

divers, and fifteen Avengers. With her new air group, LEXINGTON conducted training maneuvers on June 6th, 7th, and 8th. On June 9th and 10th, Air Group 2 conducted training aboard the ship. Air Group 94 returned on the 10th, and LTJG Richard C. Posterick of VF-94 made the 20,000th landing in an F6F. By June 13th, LEXINGTON was again on her way to the forward area as part of TG 12.4. The group proceeded to Leyte, Philippine Islands, making a one-day strike against Wake Island on the way. One hundred and seventy-three sorties were flown from LEXINGTON. Additionally, four photographic sorties were flown, and a four-plane CAP was kept over the rescue submarine. Sixty-three tons of bombs, 462 rockets, and eight Tiny Tims were dropped or fired at the targets. One Hellcat and one Corsair were lost to AA fire. The rest of the trip to the Philippines was uneventful, and LEXINGTON anchored in San Pedro Bay on June 26.

When LEXINGTON left the Philippines on July 1, there would be less than two months before hostilities would cease. The next time she dropped anchor, it would

LEXINGTON's radars are shown in this photo taken in November 1944. The number keys are as follows: 4-fire control, 10-air search and height finder, 12-radar test equipment, 13-surface search, 15 & 22-homing beacon, 21 & 23-air search, and 26-ID. All other numbers are radio communications antennas. (National Archives)

be in Tokyo Bay. But these would be busy days as the action was now taking place over Japan itself. LEXINGTON was operating as part of Task Group 38.1 under Rear Admiral T. L. Sprague. His flag was in USS BENNINGTON, CV-20. Two other task groups comprised Task Force 38. As the force moved northward toward the Japanese islands, intensive training was conducted for nine days. Then on the tenth day, Task Force 38 struck the Tokyo area. LEXINGTON's aircraft struck airfields north of the city with a mission to destroy aircraft on the ground and in the air. But throughout the raids, the Japanese refused to take to the air to defend their homeland. No enemy planes ever approached close enough to the ship to cause its guns to open fire. The Japanese had dispersed and concealed their aircraft, making the job of finding and destroying them very difficult. It meant that attacking planes had to fly low over the target area, and, as a result, losses mounted from AA fire. Bad weather also hampered flying operations.

On July 14, LEXINGTON's aircraft covered the battleship and cruiser bombardment of the Imperial Iron Works at Kamaishi, which was the first surface bombardment of the war against the main Japanese islands. The next day the target area was Hokkaido, then Task Group 38.1 moved south and struck the air fields north of Tokyo again. On July 18, a large scale attack was made on the battleship NAGATO at the Yokosuka Naval Base. This attack damaged but did not sink the vessel.

After withdrawing for several days to replenish and rest, attacks resumed on July 24. From a position south of Kobe, four strikes were launched against airfields, and two more were sent against the remnants of the Japanese fleet at Kure. On these strikes, hits were scored on the carriers AMAGI, ASO, IKOMA, and SHIMANE MARU, battleship/carrier ISE, and the cruisers AOBA, and OYODO. All of the carriers were sunk, and the ISE and the cruisers were hit again on the 28th. A tanker was sunk just south of Kure. On July 28th, strikes against airfields southeast of Nagoya resulted in claims of forty-one planes destroyed, sixteen probably destroyed, and twenty-six planes and two gliders damaged. Two strikes went back to finish off the ISE, AOBA, and OYODO, and each was left resting on the bottom.

After these strikes, the group moved northward some 300 miles off Honshu. It was not until August 9th that strikes were launched again. This time the targets included airfields and shipping in the northern neck of Honshu. More attacks were launched on the 13th in the Tokyo area, and LEXINGTON's CAP shot down a Jill, which proved to be the first and only airborne kill scored by Air Group 94.

After refueling on the 14th, strikes were launched against installations at Hyakurigahara, but before the second strike reached its targets, it was recalled in view of the Japanese agreement to surrender. Task Force 38 withdrew from the Tokyo area to refuel and rest. It operated in an area 200 miles southeast of Honshu, conducting routine patrols and gunnery practice. Until August 25, the task group simply marked time, awaiting further orders. On that day LEXINGTON moved to within approximately 100 miles of the coast of Honshu to begin a series of patrol missions designed to precede and accompany the initial occupation landings that were to be made in the Tokyo area. One of the primary goals was to locate prisoner-of-war camps and drop supplies to them. These missions to support the occupation forces and supply the POW camps continued for sixty-one days. During this time, LEXINGTON was detached from TG 38.1, and reported for duty in TG 38.3 on August 31. On that day, Vice Admiral Sherman brought his flag on board the LEXINGTON.

On September 4, LEXINGTON was detached from TG 38.3, and the following afternoon she set a precedent for fleet carriers by entering Tokyo Bay. As she dropped anchor, she came to a stop for the first time since she had left the Philippines on July 1. After embarking the Marine Detachment that had been on the beach since August 30,

This plaque has been placed in the superstructure near where the aircraft making the suicide dive struck the ship. It remains there today for all to see, marking the spot and date where the LEXINGTON received the greatest amount of damage and suffered the greatest loss in lives during the war.

LEXINGTON departed Tokyo Bay on September 6th and rejoined the task group which had been redesignated TG 38.2 on September 5. LEXINGTON reentered Tokyo Bay with the Task Group on September 10 for a period of rest and replenishment. She departed again on the 15th to continue patrols off Honshu.

Except for one replenishment period, LEXINGTON continued to conduct patrols until December 3, 1945. Then she set sail for home, arriving at the San Francisco Naval Shipyard on December 15. She was moved to Seattle in May 1946 to be deactivated, then was decommissioned on April 23, 1947. LEXINGTON was placed in the Pacific Reserve Fleet at the Puget Sound Naval Shipyard for a well deserved rest that was to last until 1953.

USS LEXINGTON
WORLD WAR II CHARACTERISTICS (As Built--1943)

Length (overall)	872 feet
Length (waterline)	820 feet
Beam (overall)	147 feet 6 inches
Beam (waterline)	93 feet
Displacement (standard)	27,100 tons
Displacement (full load)	33,000 tons
Draft (standard)	23 feet
Draft (full load)	28 feet 6 inches
Flight Deck	862 x 108 feet
Hangar Deck	654 x 70 feet
Hangar Deck Height	17 feet 6 inches
Elevators	2 centerline and 1 deck edge
Catapults	1 ea H-4 (1)
Arresting Gear	Mk 4
Machinery	8 B & W Steam Boilers
Shaft Horsepower	150,000
Speed (design)	33 knots
Crew (officers/enlisted)	275/2365 (2)

(1) A second H-4 catapult was installed later.
(2) Includes embarked air group, numbers are approximate and varied during the war.

The USS LEXINGTON has received the following awards:

The Presidential Unit Citation

The American Area Service Medal

The Asiatic-Pacific Area Campaign Service Medal with eleven battle stars

The World War II Victory Medal

The Navy Occupation Service Medal

The National Defense Service Medal

The Armed Forces Expeditionary Service Medal

The Philippine Liberation Campaign Ribbon with two stars

The Republic of the Philippines Presidential Unit Citation Badge

MODERNIZATION

The newly commissioned and modernized USS LEXINGTON leaves the pier with a part of her crew mustered on deck. Several details are noteworthy in this photograph and the one on the next page. C-11 steam catapults are installed, and they extend almost all the way back to the new island. However, note that there are no catapult overruns at this time. The forward elevator is still rectangular in shape, as is the port side elevator. There is a wedge-shaped portion of the flight deck forward of it that did not move with the elevator. Five-inch/38 and three-inch/50 guns are located in sponsons on either side of the forward end of the flight deck. The design of the hurricane bow is clearly shown here. The ESSEX class carrier to the stern of the LEXINGTON is the SHANGRI-LA, CVA-38, which received essentially the same conversion as the LEXINGTON. In the center of the background is the USS MIDWAY, CVA-41, and in the far background is the USS CORAL SEA, CVA-43. (National Archives)

When the USS LEXINGTON was recommissioned in 1955, she was practically a new ship. Looking at her features, it was hard to believe that she was actually the same LEXINGTON that had participated in the major carrier battles of World War II. In order to relate to the modernization that the LEXINGTON underwent, it is first necessary to understand how it fit into the conversion programs that the ESSEX class went through beginning in 1948. To the casual observer, it might have appeared that these ships received a new superstructure, an angled deck, an enclosed hurricane bow, and a much-reduced gun armament. The modernization programs were much more complex than this, and a full explanation would fill many volumes. Each SCB conversion program differed from the others with respect to what improvements were made, and specific details varied from ship to ship.

The dawn of the jet age, which was already beginning as World War II came to an end, caused a need for major changes in carrier design. In fact, it jeopardized the very existence of carrier aviation. With their high speeds, introduction of swept wings, tricycle landing gear, and other new features, jets could not operate on carriers unless drastic changes were made. For example, their slow acceleration on take off meant that catapults must be used, and their increasing weights meant that the catapults had to be stronger than those in service. Arresting gear, flight decks, and elevators also had to be stronger. Barriers that had been used to stop propeller-driven aircraft that missed the arresting cables simply would not work for jets, so a new type of barrier had to be developed. Nuclear weapons required new storage and handling facilities. Jets were thirsty, so more aviation fuel had to be carried, and with both jets and piston engines on board, both types of fuel had to be carried in addition to the fuel oil for the ship. The new requirements facing the carrier designers in the 1950s were awesome, and the ultimate solution was the design of the large-deck super carriers that began with the USS FORRESTAL, CVA-59.

This view shows the aft port gun sponson which had two five-inch/38 guns, but no three-inch dual mount. Two single five-inch/38 mounts and a dual three-inch/50 mount were on the opposite side, and this differed from the arrangement on several other ESSEX class conversions. Some carriers had only one five-inch gun aft and starboard, and no three-inch mount. Note the two three-inch/50 mounts on the fantail. The dark boxy items along the catwalks are rafts. In order for the carrier to handle heavier aircraft, there is a reinforced darker area that is noticeable on the flight deck that begins inside the aft **16** *and extends forward. There are six arresting cables installed at this time. Note how the starboard elevator is angled upward.* (National Archives)

But it is a tribute to the design of the ESSEX and MIDWAY classes that they could be converted into modernized jet carriers that would serve through the war in Vietnam.

Modernization of the ESSEX class began in 1948 with the SCB-27A program. SCB stood for Ship Characteristic Board. It was this program that provided the new superstructure, but the axial deck and open bow remained. The USS ORISKANY, CV-34, was completed to these standards after work had been suspended on her at the end of World War II. Less noticeable than the new island was the H-8 hydraulic catapults that could launch a 62,500 pound aircraft at a speed of 70 miles per hour. Blast deflectors for the new jets were located at the aft end of the catapults. The gun armament was changed considerably. While ORISKANY had a few 20mm Oerlikons, she was the only SCB-27A ship to have them. There were no dual five-inch mounts on the flight deck anymore, nor were there any guns on the superstructure. All weapons consisted of five-inch/38s, and three-inch/50s on the edges of the flight deck, the bow, stern, and in tubs on the starboard side. Ready rooms for the pilots were located below the hangar deck, and an escalator was added to the starboard side to bring them quickly up to the flight deck. These were the main features of SCB-27A, and additionally, there were other lesser features that included radar, communications, and other electronics systems. The ESSEX, YORKTOWN, HORNET, RANDOLPH, WASP, BENNINGTON, KEARSARGE, and LAKE CHAMPLAIN all underwent the SCB-27A program.

Second was the SCB-27C conversion that included all of the SCB-27A features, but added C-11 steam catapults instead of the H-8 hydraulic units. These catapults could launch a 70,000 pound aircraft at 125 miles per hour. The aft elevator was moved to the starboard side of the ship, strengthening the landing area, and providing a larger, stronger elevator in the process. Again, gun armament consisted of five-inch/38s and twin 3-inch/50s. A blister was added at the waterline, increasing the beam to 103 feet. The arresting gear was strengthened. The axial deck and open bow still remained on the SCB-27C ships. INTREPID, TICONDEROGA, and HANCOCK received the SCB-27C conversion.

The SCB-125 conversion was the most dramatic modernization done on the ESSEX class carriers. It involved the addition of the angled deck and enclosed bow. Mark 7 arresting gear was installed. Pri-fly, the flight control area, was installed at the aft end of the superstructure well above the flight deck. All SCB-27A ships except the LAKE CHAMPLAIN went through a second yard period to receive the SCB-125 conversion. The ORISKANY received a slightly different SCB-125A, which included the addition of C-11 steam catapults, but the rest of the SCB-27A ships retained their hydraulic H-8 catapults. All three of the SCB-27C ships also went

Taken on September 16, 1955, this view shows the angled deck and catapults to good effect. Notice how the long catapults are set at an angle, rather than running parallel to the centerline of the ship. Flight deck markings were yellow. According to a crewmember aboard the LEXINGTON who has been around long enough to remember, the flight deck was gray at this time. (National Archives)

through a second yard period to receive the SCB-125 conversion. Three additional ships, LEXINGTON, BON HOMME RICHARD, and SHANGRI-LA received both the SCB-27C and SCB-125 conversions in one yard period. Gun armament varied from ship to ship, but consisted of the five-inch and three-inch guns as before. Fire control directors included the Mk-37, Mk-25, and Mk-56. As the years passed, both the number of guns and directors would be reduced in order to lessen topside weight. Although the flight decks were strengthened, they were not armored, and the wood planking remained visible after the conversion.

A less noticeable modernization was the SCB-144 program that was first applied to the SCB-27A ships. These carriers, with their hydraulic catapults, could no longer serve as CVAs, and had been reclassified as CVSs. The SCB-144 program was part of the FRAM II (Fleet Rehabilitation and Modernization) effort that effected many ships in the Navy. It was designed to increase their abilities in anti-submarine warfare. SCB-144 included the installation of an SQS-23 sonar in a dome mounted in the bow. A third anchor was located at the point of the bow, and its associated equipment was installed in the forecastle. The combat information center (CIC) was modified so that it was better suited to the ASW role. Later, INTREPID also received a FRAM II modernization.

By studying photographs of the various ships, a person can see the differences between them. Radar fits, gun locations, and other details varied considerably. What is not always so noticeable is the differences in the shapes of the hurricane bows. The first ships so fitted had a definite angle to them just below the secondary conn. Later ships had bows that were more rounded. The catwalks on the sides of the ships at the bow differed. LEXINGTON and SHANGRI-LA had similar bows that were different in details from all other ESSEX class modernizations. Installation of catapult overruns, types of blast

By February 1956, small catapult extensions or bridle catchers had been added to the forward end of the flight deck. Notice also the middle two port holes that had been added to the lower row on the hurricane bow. The top row is for the secondary conn. Details along the port side of the ship are visible here. (National Archives)

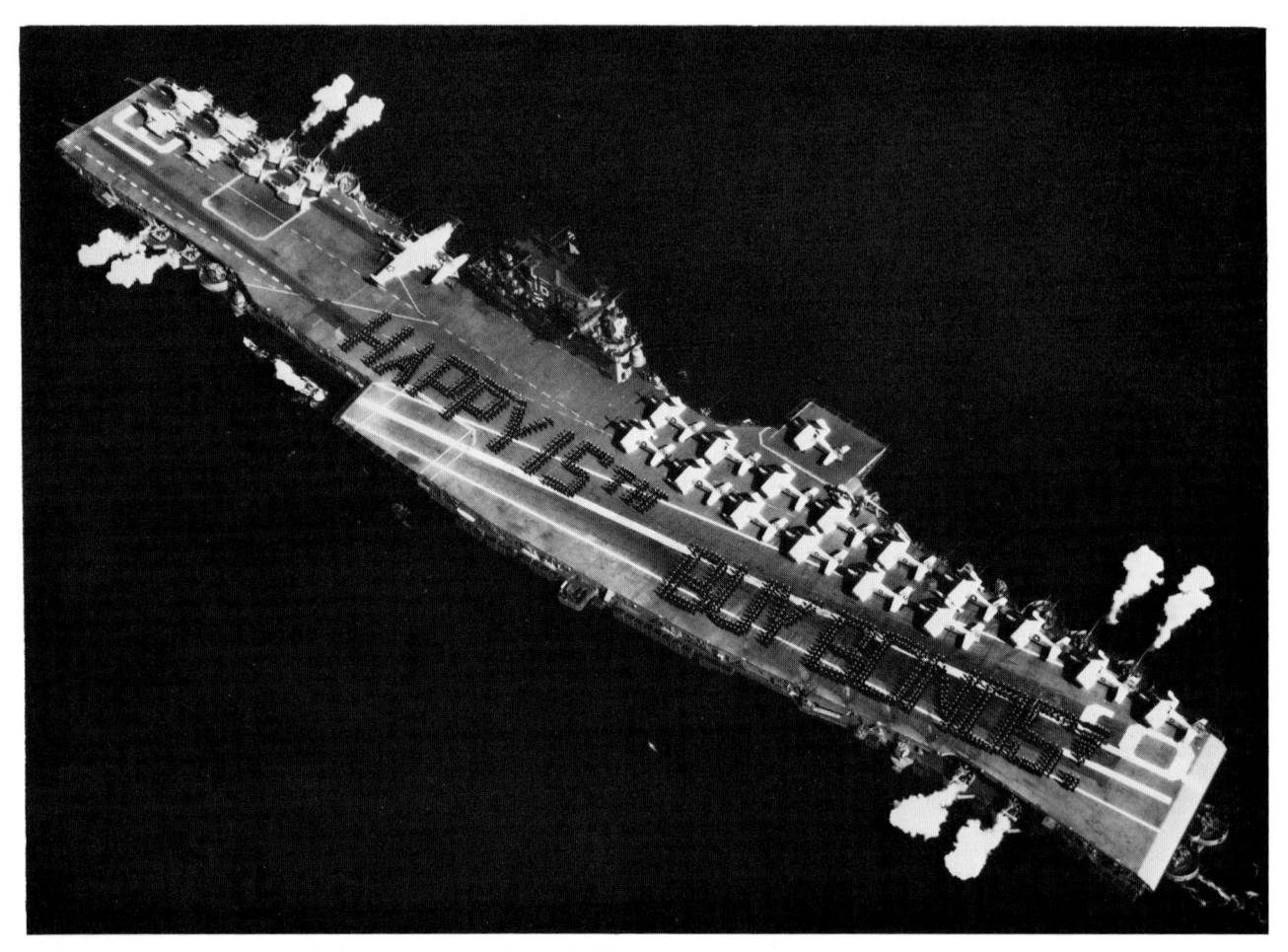

*Although the crew has made the effort to spell out **HAPPY 15th BUY BONDS!**, what is important about this photograph is that it shows the gun armament fitted to the ship upon her recommissioning. All eight five-inch/38 guns are firing. The twin three-inch/50 mounts are visible on both forward sponsons and in the starboard aft sponson. The two three-inch mounts are also visible on the fantail. Aircraft visible on the flight deck include four F7U Cutlasses forward, with four F9F Cougars parked behind them. A North American Savage is on the starboard catapult. All other aircraft are propeller-driven Skyraiders. The early wedge-shaped part of the flight deck forward of the number 2 elevator is clearly visible in this photograph.* *(National Archives)*

deflectors, shapes and sizes of the number 1 and 2 elevators, reduction in arresting gear cables, location of cranes and boats, and many more details differed between the ships and/or were modified at different times. This is especially important to a modeler who wants to build a specific unit of the ESSEX class at a specific point in time. To do so accurately requires an extensive amount of photographs and research. But the basic changes of the three major conversions or modernizations have been mentioned here, and should form a basis for further study in publications more designed to cover these aspects of aircraft carriers.

The LEXINGTON was reclassified a CVA (Attack Aircraft Carrier) on October 1, 1952, while still a decommissioned ship in the Pacific Reserve Fleet. On September 1, 1953, she was moved into drydock for a major modernization that included both the SCB-27C and SCB-125 conversions mentioned above. This modernization was completed on August 15, 1955, and the ship was recommissioned. In January 1956, she returned to the yards once again for a post shakedown availability. Two months later, in March 1956, she arrived at her new home port of San Diego. She deployed to the Western Pacific with the Seventh Fleet, and made Yokosuka, one of her targets in World War II, her overseas home port. She returned to San Diego in time for Christmas.

Training exercises were conducted off the west coast during the first three months of 1957, then she made her second cruise to the Western Pacific in April. LEXINGTON and her air groups carried out training and operations in the same waters where she had fought before. She returned to San Diego in October 1957, then entered Puget Sound the following month for an overhaul that lasted until March 1958. Another cruise with the Seventh Fleet in the Far East followed the yard period, and was concluded in December. A routine of training operations off the west coast and deployments to the Western Pacific continued throughout 1959, 1960, 1961, and early 1962. In July 1962, she was ordered to replace the USS ANTIETAM as the training carrier at Pensacola, Florida.

The three-inch/50 twin mount formed the secondary gun armament on modernized ESSEX class carriers.
(U.S. Navy)

This is one of the Mk-56 radar directors for the guns. One was located near each sponson. This one remains on the USS INTREPID.

Five-inch/38 guns like these formed the main gun armament for the modernized ESSEX class carriers including the LEXINGTON. These photographs were taken on the USS INTREPID, which is now a museum in New York City.

This photograph was taken in LEXINGTON's Combat Information Center. The CIC is the nerve center of the ship.
(U.S. Navy)

Taken in March 1961, several more changes are evident in this photo. The lights added to the forward corners of the flight deck are visible. Another two were at the aft corners. The centerline elevator has been enlarged by adding a triangular section to the forward end. Although not really discernable, the port elevator has also been enlarged to include most of the former wedge-shaped piece forward of it. Both enlargements were made to allow larger aircraft like the A3D Skywarrior to be moved between decks on them. (U.S. Navy)

A T-28 Trojan is shown in the grove for landing on July 15, 1963, after LEXINGTON had assumed her duties as a training carrier. This photograph from the stern shows that when the three inch guns were removed from the fantail, the entire sponson was also removed, leaving a rounded stern. On some other ESSEX class ships, the guns were removed, but the sponsons remained. Only four arresting cables are now installed. (U.S. Navy)

After attaching the catapult and hold-back cables, the deck crew scrambles clear as an F4D Skyray, armed with Sidewinder missiles, prepares for launch. (U.S. Navy)

Deck crewmen hook up an FJ-4 Fury to the port catapult. (U.S. Navy)

The LEXINGTON celebrated her 200,000th arrested landing in April 1967. Four five-inch guns still remained on the ship at this time. (U.S. Navy)

This T-2B Buckeye made the 250,000th landing on the LEXINGTON on June 17, 1969. It was flown by Captain Wayne E. Hammett, USN, the commanding officer of the LEXINGTON, and CDR Jensen, the CO of VT-4. As this book is written, the carrier is about to double this mark! (U.S. Navy)

By the time this photograph was taken in 1978, the LEXINGTON had been reclassified as an auxiliary, AVT-16. All gun armament had been removed, and the port elevator had been sealed in the up position. (USS LEXINGTON)

Prior to relieving the ANTIETAM, LEXINGTON entered the New York Navy Shipyard for repairs, and while there, she was reclassified CVS on October 1. She was still in the shipyard when the Cuban blockade was announced, and this caused her yard period to be shortened by two weeks. Although she was ready for action if needed, the call never came, and she reported to Pensacola on December 29, 1962. She has remained there ever since, performing her duties as the Navy's training carrier. On January 16, 1969, she was redesignated CVT-16. This was changed to AVT-16 on July 1, 1978.

LEXINGTON's primary mission now is to conduct carrier qualifications for student and fleet naval aviators. Operations are conducted in the Gulf of Mexico. During the spring, summer, and fall, she steams off the coast of Corpus Christi, Texas, and Pensacola, Florida. During the winter she shifts to the Key West operating area.

Student naval aviators who are destined to fly tactical aircraft off fleet carriers are provided two opportunities during their eighteen months in the training command to qualify. Initial experience comes in the T-2C Buckeye, where they perform two touch-and-go landings and four arrested landings. They also have four catapult shots.

After about 70 to 100 hours in the T-2C, advanced training is conducted in the TA-4J Skyhawk. The qualification process in the Skyhawk includes two touch-and-goes, and six arrested landings and catapult shots.

Approximately seventy percent of LEXINGTON's carrier qualifying scenario involves training command students. The other thirty percent involves qualifying fleet replacement, regular fleet, and reserve squadrons in the A-6 and A-7. The fleet squadrons perform two touch-and-go landings, and ten arrested landings in daylight. Six more arrested landings are accomplished at night. The ship is usually at sea about two weeks each month.

One of the things that makes the LEXINGTON unique is that she is the only carrier to have women in her crew. Some reporters and other visitors to the ship seem to make a big deal of this. Certainly, it is something significant in naval aviation that should be mentioned because it is unique, but it does not deserve some of the hype it gets. The fact is that there are both officer and enlisted women in the crew. They do their jobs alongside their male counterparts, and that is all there is to it. The fact that women can do many of the jobs on an aircraft carrier should not surprise anyone. LEXINGTON's short stays at sea make this an easy routine. How such an arrangement would work on the lengthy cruises aboard fleet carriers is not a point for debate here. Suffice it to say that for LEXINGTON's crew, the women perform their duties aboard ship just as the men do.

How much longer LEXINGTON will remain in service is anyone's guess. She has already remained operational past scheduled dates of deactivation. She is presently quite capable of continuing in her mission for many years to come. All carrier aircraft now in the fleet and the USMC can operate on her flight deck except for the F-4 Phantom, F-14 Tomcat, F-18 Hornet, and the EA-6B Prowler. The determining factor for the first three is the fact that the blast deflectors are only water cooled in the center section and not the outer sections. All three sections would have to be water cooled in order for these aircraft to operate. The EA-6B is too heavy.

The LEXINGTON is the only aircraft carrier in the U.S. Navy ever to have women in its crew. This is LT Jean CacKowski, who was the first woman officer of the deck on an aircraft carrier. This photograph was taken on the bridge of the LEXINGTON. (U.S. Navy)

COMMANDING OFFICERS

Feb. 1943 - Apr. 1943	F. B. Stump
Apr. 1944 - Jan. 1945	E. N. Litch
Jan. 1945 - Nov. 1945	T. H. Robbins
Nov. 1945 - Oct. 1946*	B. E. Crow
Aug. 1955 - Oct. 1956	A. S. Heyward, Jr.
Oct. 1956 - Sep. 1957	J. W. Gannon
Sep. 1957 - Jul. 1958	B. L. Bailey
Jul. 1958 - Jun. 1959	J. R. Reedy
Jun. 1959 - Jul. 1960	S. E. Ruehlow
Jul. 1960 - Jul. 1961	S. B. Strong
Jul. 1961 - Jul. 1962	H. P. Hilton
Jul. 1962 - Jul. 1963	L. C. Powell
Jul. 1963 - Jun. 1964	J. M. Miller
Jun. 1964 - Jun. 1965	Q. C. Crommelin
Jun. 1965 - Aug. 1966	G. A. Snyder
Jun. 1966 - Aug. 1967	J. C. Heishman
Aug. 1967 - Jan. 1969	E. W. Gendron
Jan. 1969 - Mar. 1970	W. E. Hammett
Mar. 1970 - Apr. 1971	C. F. Fitton
Apr. 1971 - Dec. 1972	J. E. Davis
Dec. 1972 - Aug. 1973	C. C. Carter
Aug. 1973 - Nov. 1973	J. E. Davis
Nov. 1973 - Jul. 1975	D. E. Moore
Jul. 1975 - May 1977	T. F. Rush
May 1977 - Nov. 1978	E. B. McDaniel
Nov. 1978 - Jun. 1980	P. E. Johnson
Jun. 1980 - Dec. 1981	W. H. Greene, Jr.
Dec. 1981 - Jun. 1983	J. W. Ryan
Jun. 1983 - Dec. 1984	H. J. Bernsen
Dec. 1984 - Nov. 1986	P. M. Feran
Nov. 1986 - Present	H. G. Sprouse

*USS LEXINGTON was taken out of service in October 1946, decommissioned in April 1947, and recommissioned in August 1955.

ESSEX CLASS CARRIERS IN COMBAT

Although designed for service in World War II, and for operating the propeller-driven aircraft of the 1940s, the ESSEX class carriers also served in combat during the wars in Korea and Vietnam. They operated aircraft with ever-increasing sophistication, speed, and weight, which is a testimony to the excellent basic design of the ships and the adaptability afforded by their modernizations. The combat service of each of the ESSEX class carriers is provided in the following listings. Next to the name of each carrier is the designation for that ship at the time of the combat service.

WORLD WAR II
USS ESSEX, CV-9
USS YORKTOWN, CV-10
USS INTREPID, CV-11
USS HORNET, CV-12
USS FRANKLIN, CV-13
USS TICONDEROGA, CV-14
USS RANDOLPH, CV-15
USS LEXINGTON, CV-16
USS BUNKER HILL, CV-17
USS WASP, CV-18
USS HANCOCK, CV-19
USS BENNINGTON, CV-20
USS BON HOMME RICHARD, CV-31
USS SHANGRI-LA, CV-38

KOREAN WAR
USS ESSEX, CVA-9
USS BOXER, CVA-21
USS BON HOMME RICHARD, CVA-31
USS LEYTE, CVA-32
USS KEARSARGE, CVA-33
USS ORISKANY, CVA-34
USS ANTIETAM, CVA-36
USS PRINCETON, CVA-37
USS LAKE CHAMPLAIN, CVA-39
USS VALLEY FORGE, CVA-45
USS PHILIPPINE SEA, CVA-47

VIETNAM WAR
USS YORKTOWN, CVS-10*
USS INTREPID, CVS-11**
USS TICONDEROGA, CVA-14
USS HANCOCK, CVA-19
USS BENNINGTON, CVS-20*
USS BOXER, LPH-4***
USS BON HOMME RICHARD, CVA-31
USS ORISKANY, CVA-34
USS PRINCETON, LPH-5***
USS VALLEY FORGE, LPH-8***

*Operated in the anti-submarine role only. Did not launch strikes against land targets in Vietnam or engage in combat, but did receive the Vietnam Service Medal.

**INTREPID, although classified as a CVS at the time, deployed twice to SEA as an attack carrier, and launched strikes against the North Vietnamese. She was the only CVS to do so.

***Delivered troops and supplies. Did not engage in combat, but did receive Vietnam Service Medal.

**USS LEXINGTON CHARACTERISTICS
AS MODERNIZED SCB-27C/-125, 1955**

Length (overall) .... 894 feet 6 inches
Length (waterline) .... 820 feet
Beam (overall) .... 166 feet 10 inches
Beam (waterline) .... 103 feet
Displacement (standard) .... 33,000 tons
Displacement (full load) .... 43,000 tons
Speed .... 30.5 knots
Draft .... 30 feet 4 inches
Length of Angled Deck .... 520 feet
Elevators (centerline) .... 1 ea, 70 x 44 feet
Elevators (deck edge) .... 2 ea, 56 x 44 feet
Catapults .... 2 ea, C-11 steam
Crew (officers/enlisted) 335/3185*

*Includes embarked air group. Numbers varied slightly from time to time.

USS LEXINGTON CHARACTERISTICS-PRESENT

Length (overall) .... 910 feet
Length (waterline) .... 820 feet
Beam (overall) .... 166 feet 10 inches
Beam (waterline) .... 103 feet
Draft .... 30 feet
Displacement (full load) .... 42,000 tons
Speed .... 30 knots
Range .... 4131 miles
Engines .... Four Westinghouse Steam Turbines
Boilers .... Eight Babcock & Wilcox
Catapults .... 2 ea C-11 steam
Elevators .... One centerline & one deck edge
Crew (officer/enlisted) 75/1368*

*Ship's crew only. No air group is embarked.

ESSEX CLASS POST-WAR MODERNIZATIONS, RECLASSIFICATIONS, AND FINAL FATES

Note: A number of sources on these ships have shown the modernizations, conversions, and fates of these ships through the use of tables. However, because of the many variations between the ships, the tables are often confusing and are full of footnotes. Below is a listing of all of the ESSEX class carriers with a summary of their post-war modernizations and final fates. This format should more adequately and clearly show pertinent information for each ship.

CV-9, ESSEX
SCB-27A begun; January 1948
Recommissioned; September 1951
Reclassified CVA; October 1952
SCB-125 completed; January 1956
Reclassified CVS; March 1960
SCB-144 FRAM II; 1962
Decommissioned; December 1969
Stricken; July 1973

CV-10, YORKTOWN
SCB-27A begun; February 1951
Reclassified CVA; October 1952
Recommissioned; January 1953
SCB-125 completed; October 1955
Reclassified CVS; September 1957
SCB-144 FRAM II; 1966
Decommissioned; June 1970
Museum at Patriot's Point, SC

CV-11, INTREPID
SCB-27C begun; September 1951
Reclassified CVA; October 1952
Recommissioned; October 1954
SCB-125 completed; February 1957
Reclassified CVS; March 1962
SCB-144 FRAM II; 1965
Decommissioned; March 1974
Museum at New York, NY

CV-12, HORNET
SCB-27A begun; June 1951
Reclassified CVA; October 1952
Recommissioned; September 1953
SCB-125 completed; August 1956
Reclassified CVS; July 1958
SCB-144 FRAM II; 1965
Decommissioned; June 1970

CV-13, FRANKLIN
Never placed in post-war service
Reclassified CVA; October 1952
Reclassified CVS; July 1953
Reclassified AVT-8; May 1959
Stricken; October 1964

CV-14, TICONDEROGA
SCB-27C begun; July 1951
Reclassified CVA; October 1952
Recommissioned; September 1954
SCB-125 completed; January 1957
Reclassified CVS; October 1969
Decommissioned; September 1973

CV-15, RANDOLPH
SCB-27A begun; June 1951
Reclassified CVA; October 1952
Recommissioned; July 1953
SCB-125 completed; February 1956
Reclassified CVS; March 1969
SCB-144 FRAM II; 1961
Decommissioned; February 1969

CV-16, LEXINGTON
SCB-27C/-125 begun; July 1952
Reclassified CVA; October 1952
Recommissioned; August 1955
Reclassified CVS; October 1962

Reclassified CVT; January 1969
Reclassified AVT; July 1978
Still Active

CV-17, BUNKER HILL
Never placed in post-war service
Reclassified CVA; October 1952
Reclassified CVS; July 1953
Reclassified AVT-9; May 1959
Stricken; November 1966
Used as electronics test ship for Naval Electronics Laboratory

CV-18, WASP
SCB-27A begun; September 1948
Recommissioned; September 1951
Reclassified CVA; October 1952
SCB-125 completed; December 1955
Reclassified CVS; November 1956
SCB-144 FRAM II; 1964
Decommissioned; July 1972

CV-19, HANCOCK
SCB-27C begun; July 1951
Reclassified CVA; October 1952
Recommissioned; February 1954
SCB-125 completed; November 1956
Decommissioned; January 1976

CV-20, BENNINGTON
SCB-27A begun; October 1950
Reclassified CVA; October 1952
Recommissioned; November 1952
SCB-125 completed; April 1955
Reclassified CVS; June 1959
SCB-144 FRAM II; 1963
Decommissioned; January 1970

CV-21, BOXER
Remained in service after WW-II
Reclassified CVA; October 1952
Reclassified CVS; November 1955
Reclassified LPH-4; January 1959
Decommissioned; December 1969

CV-31, BON HOMME RICHARD
Recommissioned; January 1951
Reclassified CVA; October 1952
Decommissioned; May 1953
SCB-27C/-125 completed; November 1955
Recommissioned; November 1955
Decommissioned; July 1971

CV-32, LEYTE
Remained in service after WW-II
Reclassified CVA; October 1952
Reclassified CVS; July 1953
Decommissioned & reclassified AVT-10; May 1959

CV-33, KEARSARGE
Decommissioned; June 1950

Recommissioned; February 1952
SCB-27A completed; March 1952
Reclassified CVA; October 1952
SCB-125 completed; January 1957
Reclassified CVS; October 1958
SCB-144 FRAM II; 1962
Decommissioned; February 1970

CV-34, ORISKANY
Commissioned; September 1950
(Commissioned as SCB-27A)
Reclassified CVA; October 1952
SCB-125A completed; May 1959
Decommissioned; May 1976

CV-36, ANTIETAM
Recommissioned; January 1951
Reclassified CVA; October 1952
Received angled deck but no
SCB modernization; December 1952
Reclassified CVS; July 1953
Decommissioned; May 1963

CV-37, PRINCETON
Recommissioned; August 1950
Reclassified CVA; October 1952
Reclassified CVS; November 1953
Reclassified LPH-5; March 1959
Decommissioned; January 1970

CV-38, SHANGRI-LA
Recommissioned; May 1951
Decommissioned; September 1952
Reclassified CVA; October 1952
SCB-27C/-125 completed; January 1955
Recommissioned; January 1955
Reclassified CVS; July 1969
Decommissioned; July 1971

CV-39, LAKE CHAMPLAIN
SCB-27A begun; August 1950
Recommissioned; September 1952
Redesignated CVA; October 1952
Decommissioned; January 1966

CV-40, TARAWA
Recommissioned; February 1951
Reclassified CVA; October 1952
Reclassified CVS; January 1955
Decommissioned & reclassified AVT-12; May 1960

CV-45, VALLEY FORGE
Reclassified CVA; October 1952
Reclassified CVS; November 1953
Reclassified LPH-8; July 1961
Decommissioned; January 1970

CV-47, PHILIPPINE SEA
Reclassified CVA; October 1952
Reclassified CVS; November 1955
Decommissioned; December 1958

LEXINGTON COLORS

Flight Ops, USS LEXINGTON, May 1987. This photograph shows TA-4J Skyhawks in various phases of operations on the carrier. At left, one aircraft is hooked to the catapult, while others wait their turn behind the jet blast deflector. Another Skyhawk is about to touch down in the landing area. In the foreground, a deck crewman, known as a "bridle runner," drags a catapult bridle back down the deck to the launching area. These bridles weigh about 120 pounds.

732 gets the signal to launch.

VT-7's commander's aircraft has just landed, and is about to be unhooked from the arresting gear.

Since the TA-4J does not have nose wheel steering, a crewman must attach a bar to the nose wheel and guide the aircraft on the deck. Since the pilot cannot see this man, he must pay careful attention to other crewmen who give him hand signals on where to move the aircraft. If the man with the bar were to fall, it would be quite serious.

33

An A-6E from VA-42 is about to launch from the starboard cat.

Wheels smoke as an EA-6A touches down.

This A-6E has just made a touch-and-go, and is airborne again after passing over the angled deck of the carrier.

This T-2C was painted in special colors in celebration of 75 years of Naval Aviation.

A more conventionally marked T-2C has just stopped and had the hook freed from the arresting cable. Because the intakes are located so low on the Buckeye, screened covers are placed over them to protect against foreign object damage or FOD.

One of the largest aircraft to operate on the LEXINGTON is the C-2 Greyhound. This aircraft is from VRC-40.

VA-172, the east coast RAG A-7E unit, conducts its carrier qualifications on the LEXINGTON. This photograph was taken in September 1986.

Reserve A-7E squadrons also conduct their qualifications on the LEX. The aircraft in the foreground is from VA-204, based at NAS New Orleans, and the one in the background is from VA-205 out of NAS Atlanta.

HC-16 provides SAR helicopter support to the LEXINGTON. This H-3 is shown taking off from the ship to cover air operations. In performing this mission, the Sea King will fly orbits on the starboard side of the ship, while the aircraft fly their patterns on the port side.

With its rotors and tail section folded for storage, this H-3 is about to be lowered to the hangar deck. These helicopters also perform some duty shuttling passengers and equipment between the ship and the shore, but most of that job is done by the LEX COD.

FLY-AROUND

This photograph shows an overall view of the LEXINGTON as she appeared in May 1987. The flight deck markings and other details are visible. The photograph was taken from the USS INDEPENDENCE C-1 COD as it prepared to land on the ship.

Above center: Good details of the starboard side of the ship are seen here. A TA-4J is right over the fantail, and is about to land. The C-1 from the USS INDEPENDENCE is about to be launched from the starboard cat. Another TA-4J and an A-6E are on the deck. This photograph, and those on the following page, were taken by the author from the SAR helicopter.

Right: With the last aircraft safely down, the helicopter passes to the stern to provide a view of the carrier from this angle. Lights on the Fresnel Lens System are clearly visible.

36

The port side of the ship is seen here.

This closer view shows details of the superstructure and the sealed-up port elevator. The opening below the elevator is also sealed, with only a small door remaining. The walls of the former opening are not movable.

A photograph from almost head-on shows the bow and forward flight deck of the carrier. The white cord hanging off the port bow is part of the bridle catching gear for the port cat.

37

MARKINGS

Left and right side views of the superstructure are shown here. On the starboard side, the **16** is visible, as are the ribbons located on the bridge. A close-up of the ribbons appears below. On the port side, the **16** is again visible, as are two blue and white flags with **SIGS** printed below them in yellow. A warning to flight deck personnel is painted lower on the superstructure in yellow.

This is a close-up looking up at the ribbons that are located on LEXINGTON's bridge.

The nickname "Blue Ghost" is painted on the fantail in blue and yellow.

This overall view of the superstructure shows the colors well. Most of the lower part of the island is black, as are the mast and radars. The Navy wings of gold are painted on the forward end of the island below the bridge, and are barely visible in this photo.

38

FLIGHT DECK COLORS

The colors of the markings and details on the forward end of the flight deck are seen here. Noteworthy are the red and yellow markings around the elevator, and the yellow lines around the blast shields. The red and white lines are foul lines, the white lines are for aircraft alignment, and the white "dots" are tie-down points. The **16,** which is only at the forward end of the flight deck, is only a white outline.

This is the position where the steam pressure for the catapults is ordered. On the LEXINGTON it is located in the center of the deck.

The catapults are fired from the catwalks on the edge of the deck. This is the port position, and the one on the starboard side is the same.

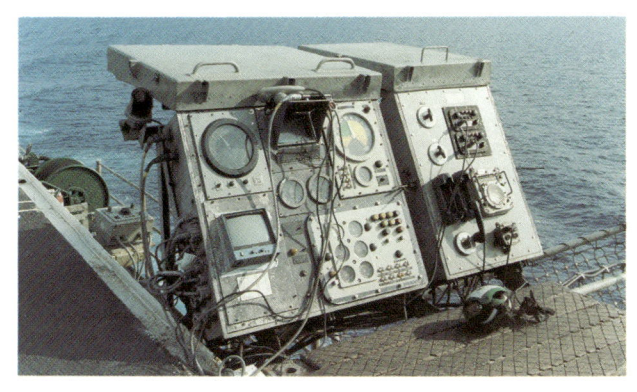

LSOs hung up their paddles long ago. Electronic gear now replaces the hand signals of yesterday. This is the LSO station on the LEXINGTON.

Tilly stands ready to retrieve aircraft that need a "lift." It stays in one position on the starboard side of the landing area while the ship is at sea, and is one of the last remaining in service.

39

USS LEXINGTON COD

Above: LEXINGTON's C-1 COD is one of the last remaining Traders in service, and is one of the most beautiful, both inside and out. The chief pilot is CDR Searcy, and he is supported by some of the nicest men in the Navy. Here the COD is shown landing aboard the ship in October 1986.

The Blue Ghost COD is hooked up to the starboard cat in preparation for the flight back to Pensacola. While the ship is at sea, the COD will make at least two trips out to the ship and back each day.

The markings on the right side of the aircraft are seen in this view taken of the aircraft while it was parked on the number 3 elevator.

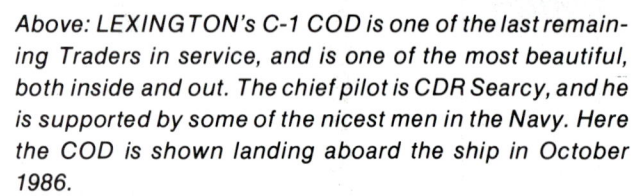

This front view shows the words **LEX COD** in white on the nose gear door.

AIR OPERATIONS

An F7U Cutlass is about to be launched from the starboard catapult in April 1956. (National Archives)

An F4D Skyray launches from the starboard cat, while another waits its turn in the lower left corner of the photograph. Three F11F Tigers are located at the far end of the port side of the flight deck. (U.S. Navy)

A T-28 makes a touch-and-go landing on June 28, 1965. Note the wooden planks of the flight deck which are clearly visible. (U.S. Navy)

An F3H-2N from VF-124 is shown here on the starboard elevator. (USS LEXINGTON)

This photograph shows an F9F Cougar from VT-25 experiencing a bolter on the LEXINGTON on February 13, 1963. It also provides a good view of superstructure details as of that date. (U.S. Navy)

Aircraft from foreign navies sometimes visit the LEXINGTON. Here a Royal Navy Buccaneer catches the wire and stops short of the starboard elevator. The photograph is dated August 16, 1965. Again note the planks of the wooden deck. (U.S. Navy)

41

LEXINGTON DETAILS
CATAPULTS

When LEXINGTON was modernized, she was fitted with two C-11 steam catapults. These were much longer than the hydraulic catapults that were installed during World War II, and the two H 8 hydraulic catapults fitted to some of the other ESSEX class conversions. These steam catapults stretched from the leading edge of the flight deck almost all the way back to the superstructure. At first there were no extensions or "horns" installed, but later small ones were located at the end of each cat below the lip of the leading edge of the flight deck. Still later, larger ones replaced these, and were blended in with the top of the flight deck. Progressively larger jet blast deflectors have also been installed. At left is an A-7E about to be launched from the port catapult. Visible are details of the three-section jet blast deflector. The port cat is not used as much as the starboard one, since landing operations cannot be conducted simultaneously with its use. It extends beyond the foul line for the landing area. At right is a look at both catapults with the blast deflector behind the starboard cat in the raised position. Each catapult is 211 feet long.

Bridles, cables, chocks and other gear are kept on the flight deck between the catapults. Different arrangements are used depending on whether the aircraft is launched with a bridle or nose tow system.

The bridle is released from this TA-4J as it steps off the end of the flight deck and into the air. The bridle will be caught by the bridle arrestor, then dragged back to the other end of the catapult by a bridle runner.

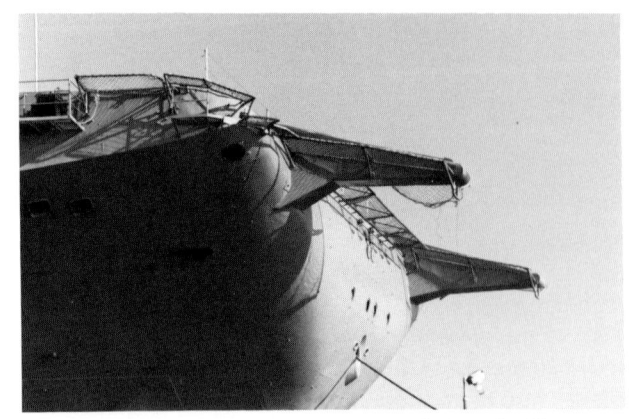

A look at the overruns that are presently installed is provided by these two photographs. Note how they are blended in to the forward end of the flight deck. Earlier overruns were below the lip of the deck.

This is the forward end of the port catapult. The cables and white cord that run along side of the catapult, then make a right angle and go off the deck, are part of the bridle arrester that keeps it from going off the ship. It is then dragged back to the hook-up end of the catapult by one of the crewmen.

A TA-4J is shown under tension on the starboard catapult. The catapult is fired by the man in the catwalk.

This is the extreme aft end of the catapult where the holdback assembly is attached to the deck. A breakable holdback T-bar is attached to the end of the holdback assembly, and is inserted into one of the cleats seen here. Which cleat is used depends on the type of the aircraft. Aircraft types are marked by the appropriate cleats, and these markings still show aircraft like the F7U, F9F, F11F, F4D, and others that have long since left the inventory. It is an interesting study in the history of various aircraft types that have operated aboard the USS LEXINGTON.

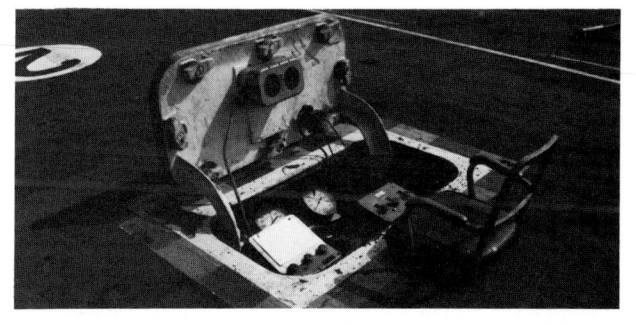

*The steam pressure is ordered at this position in the center of the flight deck. The words **CAT GRIP** painted on the hatch have an interesting meaning. A pilot pushes the throttle all the way forward with his left hand as he is about to launch. However, the acceleration of the aircraft on the catapult can cause the hand to be jerked to the rear, thus cutting the power at the worst possible moment. There is a cat grip in front of the throttle that the pilot holds on to in order to prevent his hand from moving the throttle rearward. Therefore, the throttle remains forward at full power during the launching. The sign is to remind the pilot to grab the cat grip. Note that in the close up photos of the flight deck, the non-skid covering that has been placed over the wood deck is visible. However, in many places on the deck it is still possible to see the wood planks below the covering.*

43

LANDING AREA & ARRESTING GEAR

This photograph was taken from the extreme aft end of the flight deck, and looks straight down the centerline stripe of alternating yellow and white segments.

A purchase cable inspection was being conducted on the arresting gear when this photograph was taken. The landing area is bordered by double white lines. The thin red and white foul line is visible to the starboard side of the landing area. Nothing and no one may be across this line when an aircraft is landing.

The aft end of the flight deck is shown in this photograph that looks from starboard to port. This area is known as the ramp or round down.

This view looks forward and right down the foul line. A man is positioned here to look down the line and determine if the deck is ready or foul during landing operations.

Red and green lights are located in this box that is positioned at the aft port end of the flight deck. It is right in front of the LSO platform, and informs the LSO if the deck is ready or foul. The aircraft will continue to fly its approach even if the deck is foul, and many times the deck will be declared ready only a second or two before a wave-off would have to be called. At other times the deck will not be ready in time, and the LSO has to wave off the aircraft, causing it to go around and try again. The small cable chute is for disposing of parts of the cables without having them fall near the screws and then being sucked into them.

When the LEXINGTON was recommissioned, she had six arresting cables, and this was later reduced to the present four. Each cable is 1-9/16th inches in diameter, and is attached to a hydraulic engine. Work is often done on the arresting gear while flight operations are not in progress. Reinforced areas, known as terminal impact pads, are located on the flight deck to protect it and the cable from wear. These pads are near the points where the cables enter the deck at the fair lead sheave. One impact pad is clearly visible in the photograph at left. It is at an angle, and crosses the two white lines. At right, another one of the pads is visible. The part of the cable that goes across the flight deck is known as the cross-deck pendant, and can be detached easily from the part that goes down to the hydraulic engines. That part is known as the purchase cable. The engines set the tension and retract the cables. Each cross-deck pendant is good for one hundred arrested landings, and records are kept accurately.

Two wire rope support leaf springs hold each cable up off the flight deck. They flatten out when an aircraft rolls over them. From the time the tail hook catches the cable until the aircraft is at a complete stop is about two seconds.

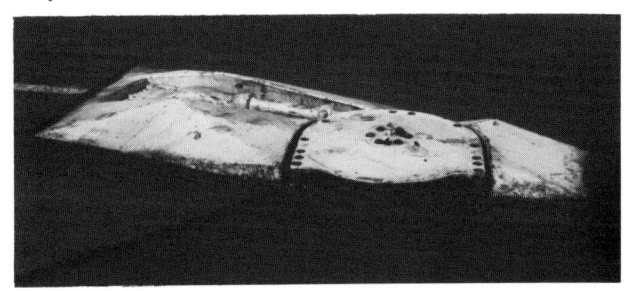

The point where the number 4 cable enters the flight deck on the starboard side is different in design than the others, allowing equipment to roll over it if necessary. Tilly is parked just forward of this point. There is no crash barrier on the LEXINGTON any longer. If an aircraft cannot get its hook down, or has some other problem that would prevent a carrier landing, it simply returns to its land base.

These two views show where cables enter the flight deck. These fair lead sheaves are fixed on the LEXINGTON, but are retractable on larger carriers. At left is the number 2 cable on the starboard side, and the attach link is visible where the cross-deck pendant is joined to the purchase cable. The impact pad absorbs the blow of this attaching link as it hits the flight deck. At right is the number 4 cable on the port side. The cable was disconnected when this photo was taken.

ELEVATORS

The forward or number 1 elevator on the LEXINGTON is the last remaining centerline elevator on any carrier in the U.S. Navy. All others are on the deck edge. It was rectangular in shape during World War II and when the ship was recommissioned. It was later enlarged at the forward end to allow it to handle larger aircraft. In the photograph at left, notice how a railing comes up around the elevator when it is in any position other than full up. At right, a TA-4J is moved into the hangar bay after being brought down on the forward elevator.

This view shows the forward elevator in the full down position. Details of the walls around the elevator well are visible.

The elevator is in the up position, and a rail is in place to prevent personnel from falling into the well. The elevator is at the forward-most end of the hangar bay.

Left: The port side or number 2 elevator is no longer functional on the LEXINGTON, having been sealed in the up position as part of the landing area. This A-7E is passing over the former elevator as it does a touch-and-go landing. The outline of the elevator is still visible.

The most often used elevator is the number 3 or starboard side elevator. In the up position, it often serves as a parking area for the COD or other aircraft. Here the COD from the USS INDEPENDENCE is shown parked on the elevator while starting its engines.

This photograph shows the starboard elevator in the up position.

Here the elevator is down, as seen during a turn to starboard. Note the protective netting around the elevator that is designed to catch any personnel that might fall or be blown off of the elevator.

This view of the number 3 elevator is looking forward across the sponson that formerly mounted a large crane. Details of the supporting framework are visible.

These two views show the elevator while the ship was in port. They reveal some of the support members underneath. In the past this elevator was angled up to a vertical position to close off the hangar bay opening, and although this capability still remains, it is no longer used.

47

LSO PLATFORM

This is the LSO panel. Notice the screens and dials that provide information. The pickle switches have been left under the left handle on top of the panel. The LSOs hold this switch above their heads when the deck is foul. When the deck is ready, they drop the hand and squeeze the button or trigger which illuminates the green light for the pilot. Each squadron provides its own LSO when it is operating on the carrier.

The LSOs stand on a wooden platform with little room to spare. Netting with canvas is located just beyond the platform. In the event of trouble, the LSOs will jump into the canvas and slide down under the platform.

These two views show the shield that protects the LSOs from the wind over the deck (WOD). The canvas and netting described above are visible again in the photograph at right.

FRESNEL LENS

These two photographs show the details of the Fresnel Lens System. Fresnel is a French word that is pronounced Free-nel, and the lens system was developed by the French. The system was adopted first by the British, then by the United States for use as an optical indicator for landings aboard aircraft carriers. The pilot knows that he is on the correct approach when a yellow light in a vertical row aligns with a stationary row of green lights. If the approach is bad, the LSO will turn on a red wave-off light. If the approach is perfect, the aircraft will catch the number three wire.

FANTAIL

The fantail of the LEXINGTON is now totally devoid of any reminder of the three-inch gun tubs and sponsons that were in place when the ship was recommissioned. Other ESSEX class modernizations had the guns removed, but the sponsons remained. The view at left is looking down at the fantail at the hangar deck level from the extreme aft end of the port catwalk on the flight deck. At right is a photograph of the stern of the ship that reveals the name **LEXINGTON** painted in black.

This view looks to port. The open door leads to the hangar bays.

The structure that supports the aft end of the flight deck is shown here. The view is looking up and to starboard.

This view is looking forward on the starboard side of the fantail.

49

SUPERSTRUCTURE & RADARS

Note the radar fit on the LEXINGTON when this photograph was taken in the early 1970s. The large radar to the left in the photo is the SPS-43. (USS LEXINGTON)

This photograph was taken from the same position as the one to the left, but shows the radar fit as it is today. The radars include the SPN-43, which is a small radar antenna mounted high and forward on the mast. The SPS-10 surface search radar is mounted below it and to port on the mast, and the SPS-40 two-dimensional air search radar is sponsored out from the top of the superstructure.

The mast is seen here from the rear. Note the whip antennas located on the superstructure as well as some of the rigging that is visible. Pri-fly is also seen below the funnel.

The superstructure is seen from behind and to the left in this view. The SPN-35 final approach radar is under the large dome at the aft end of the superstructure. It is used mostly in bad weather or at night.

The World War II superstructure was completely replaced with a new one during modernization. All modernized ESSEX class carriers except one had islands of this design, although details varied. ANTIETAM retained her original island and dual five-inch guns when she became the first U.S. carrier to be fitted with an angled deck. ORISKANY was completed after the war with this style of superstructure.

This view of the mast was taken from starboard. The small SPN-43 radar antenna that is mounted forward on the mast is visible in this photograph.

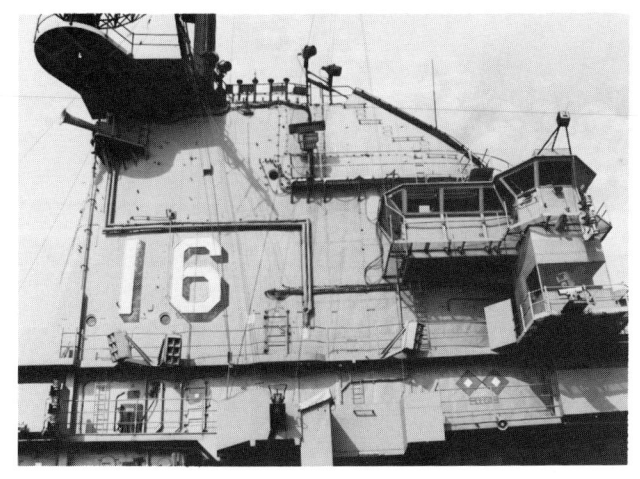

The upper portion of the port side of the superstructure is seen here. A television camera is located in the glassed-in area under pri-fly. Flight operations are recorded by several cameras. Another stationary camera is outside the glassed-in area.

Details of the SPS-40 radar are seen here. The photo is taken looking aft.

51

BRIDGE

At left is a photograph of the bridge area from below and to starboard, and at right is a view from port. The upper level is the bridge for the ship, and the lower level is the flag bridge. It is no longer used as such on the LEXINGTON.

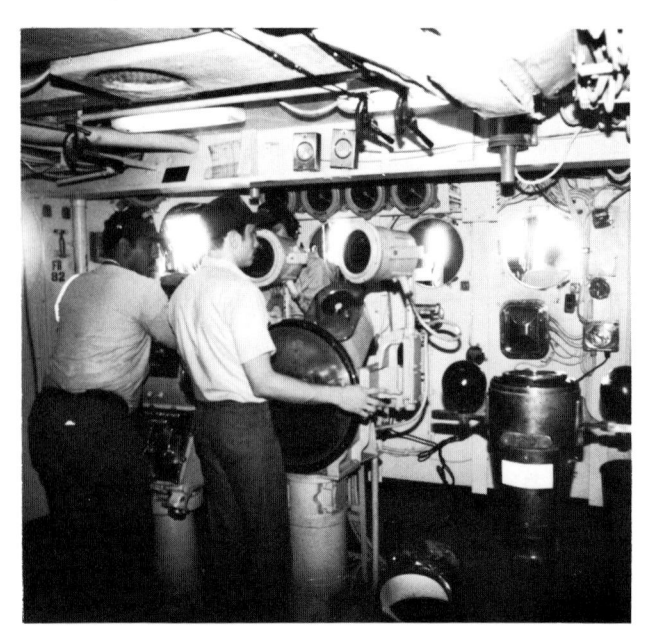

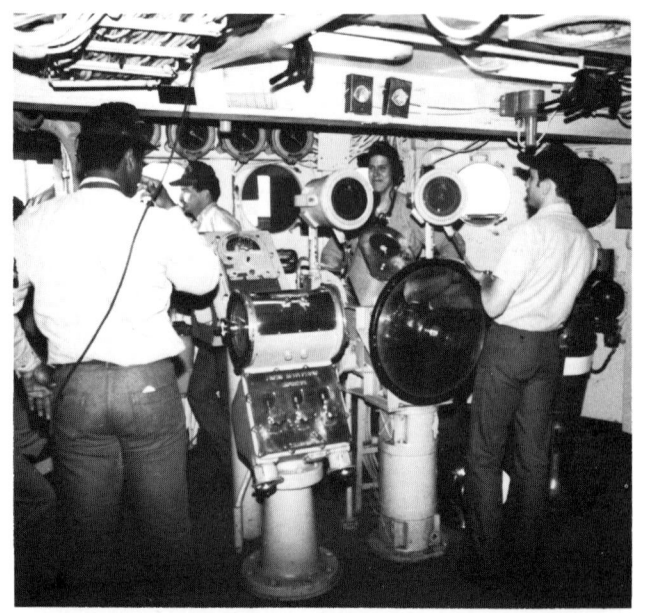

These two views show the pilot house where the ship is steered and speed is ordered. It is located just inside the bridge area, which is visible through the port holes in the photograph at left. In the photo at right is a view of the helm where the ship is steered. To the left of it is a pedestal. At the top of it is the engine order telegraph that sends signals to the engine room informing them what speed is desired. Below it is the engine revolution indicator. Engine speeds include flank, full, standard, ahead 2/3, ahead 1/3, stop, back 1/3, back 2/3, and full astern.

Right: Officers and enlisted personnel are shown at their stations on the bridge during flight operations.

PRI-FLY

Air traffic control is accomplished by pri-fly. It is located at the aft end of the superstructure, and projects far enough to the port side to provide a view of the entire flight deck.

These two photos show the inside of pri-fly. The view at left is looking to port. The two people closest to the camera are looking aft. The man standing in the light colored shirt is the Air Boss who is in charge of air operations which include all air traffic around the ship and on deck. Other personnel record launches and check settings on the arresting gear. They tell the people in the arresting gear engine rooms what type of aircraft is landing. Others control the Fresnel Lens. At right is a view taken from the forward-most part of pri-fly, and is looking aft.

This is the view from pri-fly looking down at a TA-4J that is making a landing.

The SPN-44 doppler radar is located just outside of pri-fly, and measures the aircraft's end speed as it comes in for a landing.

53

HANGAR DECK

It is not often that aircraft, other than the SAR H-3 helicopters, are kept on the hangar deck unless they have a maintenance problem. But there are exceptions. Here a T-2 Buckeye, C-1 Trader, and TA-4J Skyhawk can be seen on the hangar deck.
(USS LEXINGTON)

At left is a view looking from starboard to port at the forward end of the hangar deck. The well for the number 1 elevator can be seen at the far right. At right is a view taken at the forward-most point of the hangar deck looking aft. The A-6E in the photograph is at about the half-way point toward the other end of the hangar deck. The hangar deck can be divided into three hangar bays by large doors. The forward-most bay is bay 1, and is 144 feet long, bay 2 is 184 feet long, and the aft-most bay 3 is 236 feet long. The entire hangar deck is about 40,000 square feet in area.

With lots of room available, the hangar bays are used for jogging, basketball, and other activities. The door at the right in this photo leads out to the quarterdeck.

In the area just below the superstructure there are several insignias and other paintings that relate to the LEXINGTON and her service.

The well for the forward elevator is visible in the center of this photograph which is looking forward.

The hangar deck control station is located on the port side about two-thirds of the way back from the front. It controls the elevators and movement of all aircraft and equipment on the hangar deck.

Taken from the same spot as the photo above right, this view was taken simply by turning to the left about 45 degrees. The SAR Sea King helicopters are parked in this area of the hangar bays.

On the starboard side of the hangar deck is a shielded area marked CONFLAG STA. 2. In the past, it would have been used to direct fire-fighting efforts in the hangar bays if it had become necessary.

This TA-4J is located directly across from the opening for the number 3 elevator.

This is the aft end of the hangar deck. Fork lifts and other machinery can be seen here.

BELOW DECKS

Quarterbacks, speedy receivers, and flashy running backs get the headlines and the glamour in football. But not even the best of them could do their job without the offensive line that seldom gets mentioned. The same is true on an aircraft carrier. People in the Air Operations Department get most of the attention and the "glamour," but if it was not for the rest of the crew below decks, the ship would not function--it would not even move. All too often these crewmen, with a variety of jobs too numerous to mention, don't get much, if any, credit. A prime example is the engine room where it is very hot and cramped. At left is a burnerman on watch at one of the ship's boilers. At right is the gauge board on the number 8 boiler. There are four firerooms with two boilers each. Each boiler works at 600 psi and up to 850 degrees. The ship's four engines develop 150,000 horsepower.

This is the boiler front of the number 8 boiler. Not only do the boilers supply steam for the main engines, they also produce the steam for the turbo generators, catapults, and many other uses throughout the ship. The fuel tanks are capable of containing over 1.5 million gallons of oil to feed the boilers.

A throttleman is shown positioned at the main control gauge board.

These plates were found during work on the boilers and engines. They were installed when the ship was first built in 1941-42.

Four turbo generators and two diesel generators provide 7,000 kilowatts of electrical power. This is the electrical control and distribution panel.

This is a machine shop that can make parts that may be needed by the ship. Many parts are no longer available, and must be manufactured here. It is also interesting to note the parts from the SHANGRI-LA at the Philadelphia Navy Yard, and YORKTOWN, which is now a museum at Patriot's Point, South Carolina, have been canabilized for use on the LEXINGTON. The state of repair on the SHANGRI-LA has deteriorated badly, and, unfortunately, a crew member of the LEXINGTON was killed when a hatch fell on him while he was getting parts for his ship.

This is one of four evaporators that supply fresh and feed water for the ship. They have a production capacity of 180,000 gallons per day.

STATEROOM

These two views show the inside of an officers' stateroom. Four officers would be assigned to this stateroom. The porthole does not open to the outside of the ship, but only to the next passageway. Various pipes can be seen overhead. This particular stateroom is located under the port catapult, about even with the forward port gun sponson.

WARDROOM

Feeding the crew is another important job that goes on almost around the clock. Aboard the LEXINGTON there is an officers' mess, chiefs' mess, and enlisted mess. This is the officers' wardroom that serves everything from an early breakfast to a midnight snack. During trips to the LEXINGTON, the author was impressed by the variety, quantity, and quality of the food.

Right: This large screen television is located in a lounge next to the officers' wardroom. During flight operations, the cameras above the decks feed the action to this and other televisions below. An A-6E is seen here on the screen. In the evenings, TV programming is presented if flight operations are not in progress. Popcorn and snacks are available.

WALK-AROUND

Photographs on this page and the next three were taken in a "walk-around" the ship, mostly at the flight deck level. They show a number of the ship's details that may be of interest. These details should be particularly helpful to the modeler who may want to build a model of the LEXINGTON as she appears today. These two views show the forward catwalks, nets, railings and gun sponson on the port side of the flight deck. The view at left is looking forward, and the view at right looks aft.

At left is a view looking forward along the port edge of the angled deck. The Fresnel Lens System is visible on the side of the catwalk and deck. At right is a photograph taken from about the same position, but at the hangar deck level. It shows the overhang of the angled deck, the supporting members, and one of two boats on the LEXINGTON.

This is the aft port gun sponson. The base for one of the five-inch guns still remains.

This photograph was taken from the number three elevator, and shows the starboard quarter. A second whale boat is visible forward of the gun sponson. Note the whip antenna in the foreground that is in the lowered position.

*The whale boat was removed from its position when this photograph was taken while the LEXINGTON was in port. Note the words **LADY LEX** on the supporting cables for the boat.*

Above left and right: The aft gun sponson on the starboard side is shown here. Not all ESSEX class modernizations had this sponson, having a single five-inch gun mounted a little forward of this position instead. The barrel-like items on the sponson are Mk5 Mod2 life rafts.

One of the features of the ESSEX class modernizations was an escalator that brought pilots up to the flight deck. It was located below the superstructure. At left is a close-up of the escalator from the outside, and at right is a view looking down the escalator from the inside.

This view looks down from the aft end of the superstructure, and shows the small section of flight deck on the starboard side of the island. Equipment is stored in this area. Tractors and other ground support equipment for aircraft (commonly known as yellow gear) are parked here. The steps extending down to the right seem to lead to nowhere!

The launching station for the starboard catapult is shown here.

The forward gun sponson on the starboard side is shown here. The small catwalk in the foreground is where the starboard catapult is fired.

This is the forward-most catwalk on the starboard side of the flight deck. The non-skid surface of the flight deck is clearly visible here.

Foc'sle is a shortened form of forecastle. It is located inside the hurricane bow of the LEXINGTON, and is where the anchors are raised and lowered. Each anchor weighs fifteen tons. Two anchor chains, one nine shots, and the other twelve shots, are attached to the anchors. A shot is fifteen fathoms, and a fathom is six feet. Each chain link weighs 130 pounds. The anchors are hoisted by a windlass that is controlled by an operator in the foc'sle. These two photographs were taken inside the foc'sle and show the anchor chains to good effect. The view at left is looking forward, and the one at right looks from starboard to port.

The ship's bell is located inside the quarterdeck. It is made of solid brass, and weighs 1100 pounds. When LEXINGTON was decommissioned after World War II, the bell was removed and put on display at NAF Andrews, Maryland. It was returned to the ship in July 1981.

The quarterdeck is used by officers and chief petty officers when arriving and leaving the ship. It is traditionally a ceremonial place where dignitaries are greeted and honors rendered.

The starboard anchor is seen here. The starboard anchor is bronze in color, while the port anchor is mostly the same gray as the ship with bronze tips.

This view shows the starboard bow. Note the large vertical facing above the enclosed bow to which catwalks and a pair of whip antennas are attached. This facing, which is similar on the port side, is a major difference between LEXINGTON and most other ESSEX conversions. The facing was the same on the SHANGRI-LA and BON HOMME RICHARD, but all other ESSEX conversions were considerably different in this area.

MODELERS SECTION

AVAILABLE KITS

Only one kit exists that claims to be the LEXINGTON, and it really isn't a model that was based on the actual LEXINGTON. That kit is the Revell Model H-444, which will be discussed later. Other kits of ESSEX class carriers exist in the World War II configuration and the post-modernization, angled-deck design. Each of these can be used to model the LEXINGTON if enough work is done by the modeler to correct faults and make other specific changes that are required by a model of the LEXINGTON as opposed to another ESSEX class carrier. Some kits are better than others, and it is appropriate that we first take a brief look at each of these kits before getting into more specific information on building a model.

In the World War II configuration, the oldest and largest kit is one by Lindberg that dates back to the early 1950s when it was released as the USS WASP (CV-18). Although the WASP was a short hull carrier, the kit represents the long hull design. It has been re-released many times since then under several names including the USS ENTERPRISE (CV-6). The ENTERPRISE was not an ESSEX class carrier, but was a member of the earlier YORKTOWN class.

A more recent release is one of the USS BOXER (CV-21). The kit is in 1/520th scale, and leaves a lot to be desired. Much work would have to be done to make this a decent model of any ESSEX class carrier at any point in time. There are two rudders, whereas the real ships had only one. Openings in the sides at the hangar deck level are incorrect, there are no supports or fairings from the hull to the port side five-inch gun sponsons, the gun arrangements are wrong for any ESSEX class ship, and there are many more problems of considerable magnitude. In short, it would probably be just as easy to build a model from scratch as it would be to try to "accurize" this one. It is fair to say that this kit is a "representation" of an ESSEX class carrier rather than being a model of one. The kit comes in a motorized version, and perhaps its best use would be as a toy instead of a scale model.

Revell's INTREPID (also released as FRANKLIN) is in 1/720th scale.

The old Lindberg kit has been released numerous times, and leaves a lot to be desired. It would take almost as much work as a scratchbuilt model to turn this into a truly accurate model of the LEXINGTON (or any ESSEX class carrier) as she appeared in World War II.

The smallest ESSEX class model is in 1/720th scale, and has been released by Revell as a FRANKLIN (CV-13), kit number H-484, and INTREPID (CV-11), kit number H-462. Based on the incorrect gun arrangements and other features, it would appear that Revell based the design of this model in part on the earlier Lindberg kit. Like the Lindberg kit, this is more of a toy than a true scale model. Its detailing is not good, especially when it comes to the five-inch and 40mm guns. They do not look at all like the real thing. Again, there are two rudders instead of the correct single rudder, and the propellers are not correct. The openings in the hull at the hangar deck level are also inaccurate. For example, the scale model aircraft supplied with the kit cannot pass through the opening for the port elevator. Although it can be built as either a full hull or waterline model, it is nowhere near as good a kit as the Hasegawa offering, and is best left for beginning modelers.

Hasegawa has released two kits of World War II ESSEX class carriers in 1/700th scale. Kit number 108 is in the form of a short hull version, and kit 113 is of a long hull version. The difference between the kits is the forward end of the hull, which is the appropriate design for the ship that model is to represent. The ESSEX is the subject of kit 108, and the HANCOCK is the long hull ship in kit 113. Both of these are basically good kits, but again much work is required to build an accurate LEX-

The Hasegawa models of the ESSEX and HANCOCK are really the same model. One is for the short hull version (ESSEX), and one is for the long hull (HANCOCK). The short hull is appropriate for the LEXINGTON. This kit is far and away the best one to start with when building a model of the LEXINGTON as she appeared in World War II.

63

INGTON. Larry Gertner explains the work that must be done to kit 108 in his article, so we will not comment further on it here. His article covers all of the necessary details very well. It should be mentioned here that Hasegawa has released a kit of 1/700th scale U.S. Navy aircraft that can be used with this model. The kit number is WL 100, and it includes F4U Corsairs, SB2C Helldivers, F6F Hellcats, and TBF Avengers. All types operated from the LEXINGTON. Fujimi also released a kit of 1/700th U.S. Naval aircraft that includes SBD Dauntless dive bombers, TBF Avengers, and F4F Wildcats. The SBD operated from the LEXINGTON in 1943 and much of 1944. The F4F only operated from LEXINGTON during her shakedown cruise. These two kits of aircraft can be used to supplement the Corsairs, Hellcats, Helldivers, and Avengers that come in the kit.

There have been two major kits released of modernized ESSEX class carriers, although at least one smaller one did exist at one time. The two primary ones were by Revell and Renwal, and unfortunately, the one by Renwal is no longer available. Both of these kits will be discussed in more detail in the section covering how to build a present-day LEXINGTON.

MODELING ACCESSORIES

In the past few years, a number of sources have started producing photoetched brass and stainless steel accessories for detailing ship models. Most are commercial operations, but even IPMS/USA has offered these etchings. The parts made available on these etched sheets include everything from railings to radars, and cranes to crewmen. Even bicycles and hose reels have been included. Modelers of even modest or average ability can use these parts to greatly enhance their ship models. One producer of these photoetched parts, Gold Medal Models, has supplied us with a listing of their extensive etched sheets. Several of these will be useful to anyone building a model of the LEXINGTON in 1/700th scale using the Hasegawa kit. These include number 124B, 1/700th aircraft carrier; 127B, 1/700th aircraft parts; 129B, 1/700th extra ladders; and 115B, 1/600th and 1/700th figures. Number 106B, 1/700th naval parts will also be helpful. Further, Gold Medal Models will soon be releasing a special sheet designed for the Revell modernized ESSEX class model, which could also be used on the Renwal model. This sheet will include all of the appropriate radars used on these ships during their service, railings, props for the propeller-driven aircraft, and other small parts. It should be very worthwhile for any modeler building the Revell kit regardless of which particular ship he is modeling. A handbook on photoetching for the plastic ship modeler is also available from Gold Medal Models, and it lists other sources of photoetched ship parts. For further information, modelers can write directly to Gold Medal Models at 12332 Chapman Avenue, Number 81, Garden Grove, California 92640. Include $1.00 plus a SASE for a complete listing of the parts that they have available.

It must be kept in mind that building a ship model is not like building an aircraft model. Each ship, although a unit of a given class, has its own distinct features, and each time it goes through a major yard period, some of these features are altered, deleted, or new ones can be added. Therefore, it is important to select a specific point in time that will be used as a basis for the model. The features of the ship for that point in time are what must be represented on the model, and these may be considerably different from the features on the same ship only a few months earlier or later. It is because of this fact that the dates for many of the photographs are provided in this publication, and the changing features are pointed out in the captions. Modelers should carefully note the dates and explanations in the captions when preparing to build a model of the LEXINGTON.

BUILDING MODELS OF THE LEXINGTON
WORLD WAR II

Larry Gertner, a well known ship modeler in IPMS/USA circles, has written the following article on the best way to build a model of the LEXINGTON as she appeared in World War II. Because there was no Detail & Scale in World War II, it is not possible to include a lot of detailed photographs of the ship during that time frame as we have for the way LEXINGTON appears today. Therefore, Larry has included three pages of detailed drawings that show what needs to be done to the kit. These drawings are marked to correspond to the step-by-step instructions that he has provided. Modelers should also note the detailed photographs of the ship in World War II that have been included in this publication. Care has been taken to point out changes made to the ship as the war progressed. These photographs, along with Larry's narrative and drawings, should provide the modeler with enough information and details to build an accurate model of the LEXINGTON in World War II.

Building a World War II LEXINGTON, by Larry Gertner

Building a model of LEXINGTON in any of her wartime configurations poses one immediate problem: no such kit exists of LEXINGTON herself. However, kits do exist of ESSEX class carriers which can be modified.

I chose to start out with the Hasegawa 1/700th scale waterline kit of ESSEX (WL A108). I did so because I've been building in 1/700th scale for years, and I'm rather familiar with this particular kit. I have even written an article on modeling ESSEX herself for the IPMS Quarterly in the Fall 1982 issue. So much of what I learned then can also be applied in this case. Depending on how well you shop around, you can buy this kit for anywhere from $10.00 to $14.00.

I decided to model LEXINGTON as she appeared in October 1944. Besides her "trademark" Measure 21 Overall Navy Blue camouflage scheme, she was also unusual in receiving such late war modifications as the numerous extra 40mm quad mounts and upscaled radar fit, while keeping such earlier features as the 40mm quad forward of the flag bridge, the single 40mm quad on the fantail, and five radio masts along the starboard deck edge.

Building LEXINGTON will involve some work above and beyond merely assembling the kit's parts, but it's nothing that any ambitious modeler can't handle with the basic tools on hand. The only thing that you'll really need is a selection of white sheet styrene, such as it marketed by Evergreen or Squadron Shop. Get an assortment package that contains sheets of .010, .020, and .040 thicknesses. A razor saw might also come in handy.

Now for the author's disclaimers. The instructions that follow are based on what I've been able to piece together from a variety of sources. After all, I did not have this Detail & Scale book to work from while building my model and doing my research. I take full responsibility for any errors and misinterpretations that may follow. I am not a draftsman, but the drawings are as accurate as I can make them. In any event, I believe in building now with the information that I have available, then going back to make corrections or enhancements later if new data appears.

The written descriptions of the work to be done are keyed to the illustrations that follow. Please read through the entire text before you begin building.

PART 1, CORRECTIONS TO THE HULL AND STERN

The good news is that the starboard side appears to be accurate enough to get by with. The bad news is that the port side needs a lot of work.

Step 1. Inboard of the location of Part C-15, hangar deck level 40mm gun platform, are three hangar openings which are inaccurate. This area should be identical to the opening on the starboard side. Cut out this section from the front of the hull to the aft edge of the aftermost door, taking care not to damage the groove where Part C-15 will go. You will now have to make a new door. The drawings show my method for doing this. The rear plate is .040 plastic, and I inscribed the pseudo-rolling doors as closely together as possible. The hangar door cutout and runners are of .020 sheet styrene. As long as we are so far forward, remove the flanges from both the port and starboard sides. As a final touch, the second of the two hangar doors forward of the deck edge elevator is twice as wide as it should be. A .020 shim will bring it down to size. Once everything is dry, the next step is to attach the bow and its associated pieces.

Step 2. This section will involve the most work. Between the deck edge elevator opening and the after five-inch gun gallery sponson are three groups of seven hangar openings arranged 3-3-1. Not only are they the wrong sizes and shapes, but they are wrong in number. There should be ten openings arranged 4-3-2-1. This whole section has to be replaced. Remove the area running from 12mm before the forward edge of the foremost door all the way back to the gun sponson, and remove the first 10mm of that too. The replacement can be constructed in much the same way as in the previous step. Later, after the hull has been sanded down in Step 6, add a strip of .010 sheet 10mm long and 2mm wide forward of the first door and below the very small opening. This catwalk led to a whaleboat which can be represented by the kit's Part D-24.

Step 3. The aft five-inch gun gallery sponson is 10mm too long. On the earlier ESSEX class carriers, it did not support the quad 40mm gun tub, nor was that tub on the same level as the five-inch guns, being slightly above them instead. The extra 10mm was removed in Step 2, so now you must plate over the hole that remains. You can then take the Part D-25, gun deck, cut it down, and install it. Then build the new 40mm tub and locate it accordingly. (At this point I had better mention one of my basic rules of scratchbuilding parts. I generally form decks and bulkheads of .020 sheet. For spray shields and splinter shields I used .010 in this case. The .010 is actually too thick to be in scale, and I would rather use .005 sheet, but in this case .005 shields would be too thin in comparison to all the other moldings in the kit.) Finally, a 40mm director tub must be made from hollow tubing and positioned on Part D-25.

Step 4. The forward five-inch gun gallery, Part D-29, is almost correct, but the 40mm tub must be raised. Remove the little bit of 40mm tub overhang from it and cover the gaps with a new spray shield. Once this part has been put into place, your newly-built 40mm tub can be positioned above it. Additionally, a 40mm director tub was positioned on the gun deck.

Step 5. The hangar deck 40mm platform, Part C-15, should be supported by a massive sponson. The way I handled this was to first fit Part C-15 into place, then fiddle with rough cuts of .020 sheet beneath it. Start with the large center section, then add the ends and fare the edges into the hull when everything fits.

Step 6. Assuming that all the glue and putty has now set, sand the side smooth except for the vicinity of the deck edge elevator runners. Don't worry about all the raised detail, because much of it does not belong there. You will have to add the forward boat boom, the fore and aft gas lines, and the boat catwalk though. If you can stretch sprue, your problem is solved. I can't, so I substituted lengths of very thin brass wire. I've also done it on other carriers with thin fishing line.

Step 7. There should only be one 40mm tub on the fantail. It was offset to port with its director tub to starboard. Cut off the huge support from the hull. Fill the hole with plastic and putty, then sand it smooth. Take the Part C-13 deck, remove the starboard 40mm tub, smooth it down,

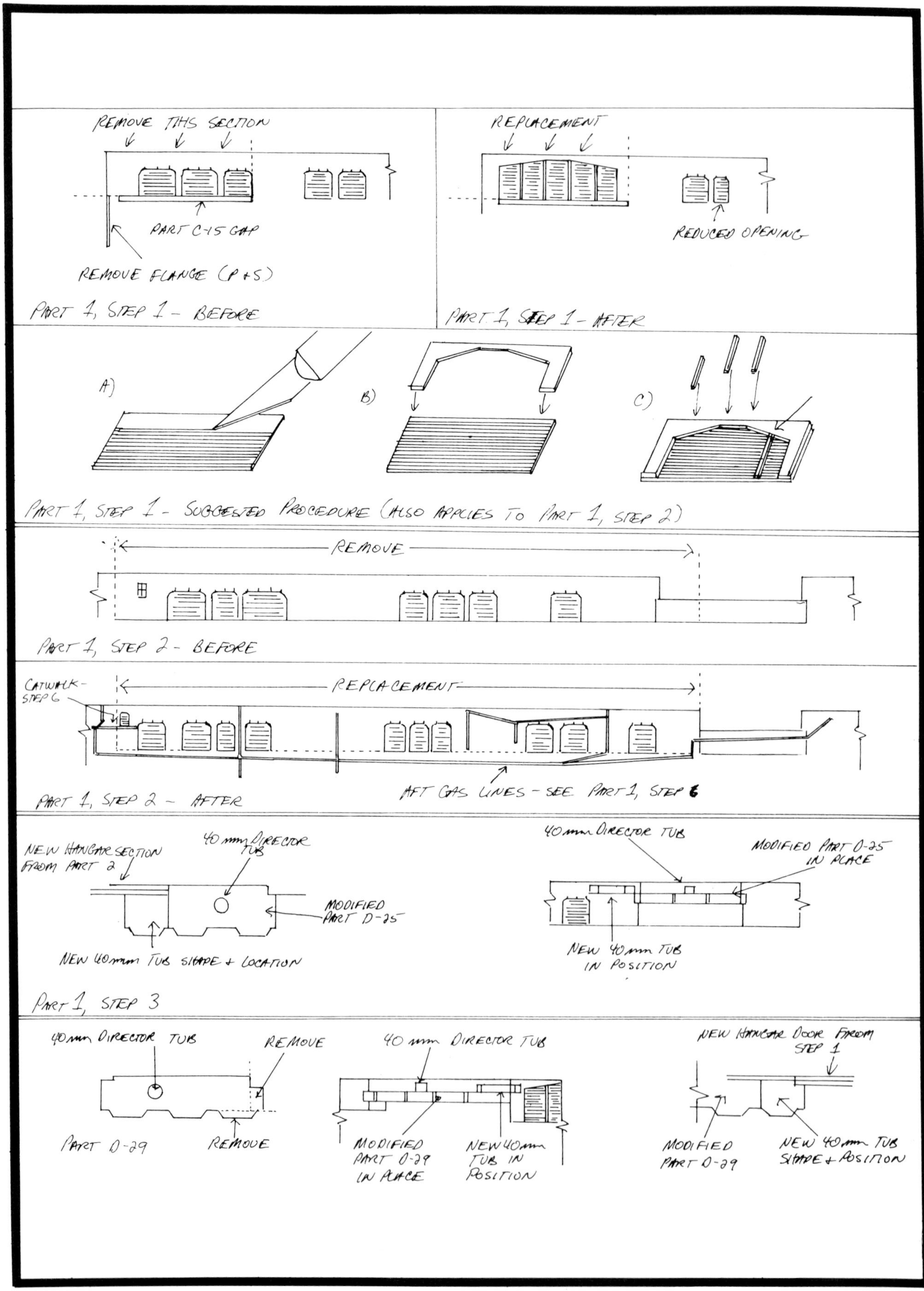
REMOVE THIS SECTION
PART C-15 GAP
REMOVE FLANGE (P+S)
PART 1, STEP 1 - BEFORE
REPLACEMENT
REDUCED OPENING
PART 1, STEP 1 - AFTER
A)
B)
C)
PART 1, STEP 1 - SUGGESTED PROCEDURE (ALSO APPLIES TO PART 1, STEP 2)
REMOVE
PART 1, STEP 2 - BEFORE
CATWALK - STEP 6
REPLACEMENT
AFT GAS LINES - SEE PART 1, STEP 6
PART 1, STEP 2 - AFTER
NEW HANGAR SECTION FROM PART 2
40 mm DIRECTOR TUB
MODIFIED PART D-25
NEW 40mm TUB SHAPE + LOCATION
40 mm DIRECTOR TUB
MODIFIED PART D-25 IN PLACE
NEW 40mm TUB IN POSITION
PART 1, STEP 3
40mm DIRECTOR TUB
REMOVE
PART D-29
REMOVE
40 mm DIRECTOR TUB
MODIFIED PART D-29 IN PLACE
NEW 40mm TUB IN POSITION
NEW HANGAR DOOR FROM STEP 1
MODIFIED PART D-29
NEW 40mm TUB SHAPE + POSITION

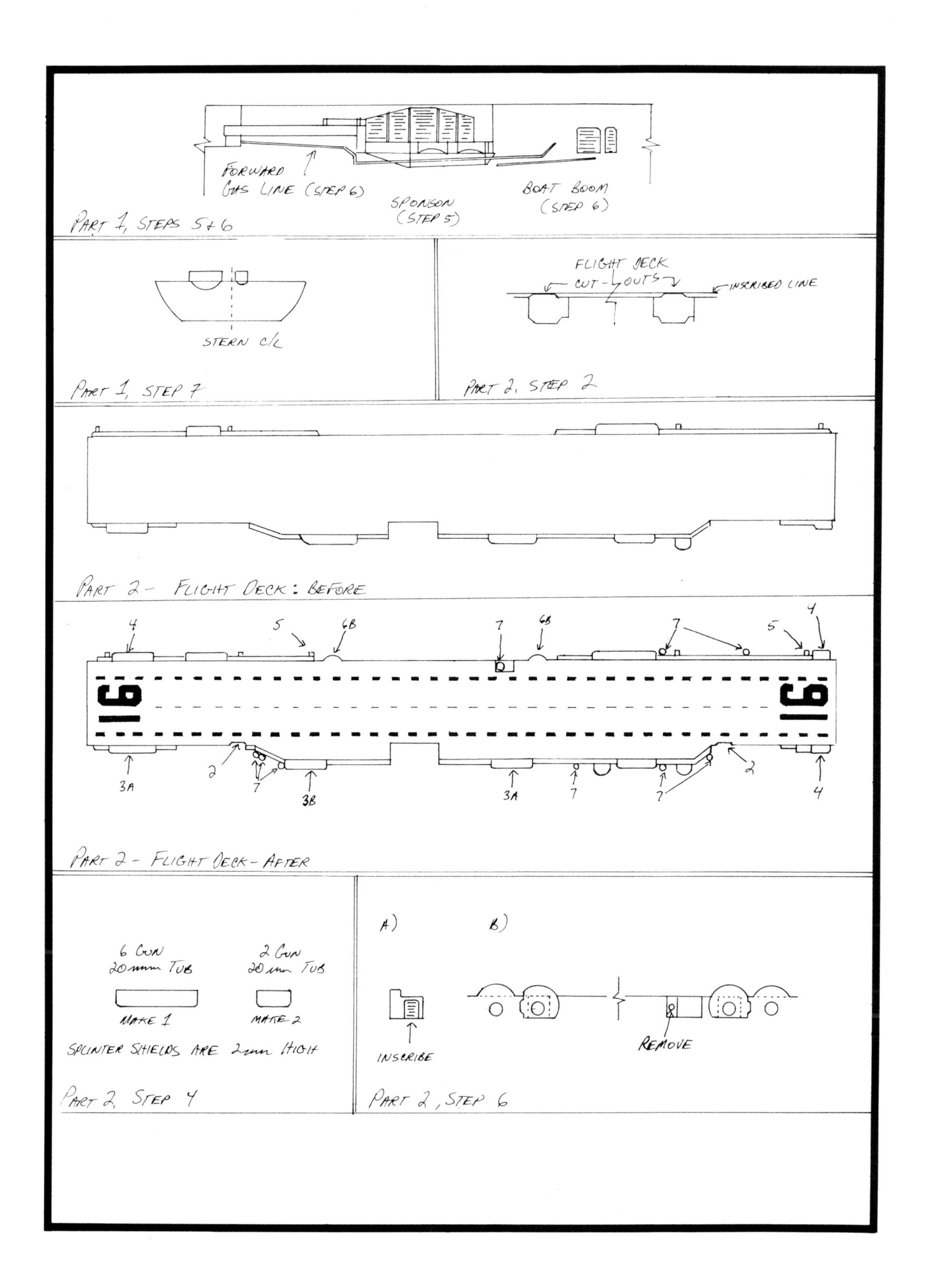

FORWARD GAS LINE (STEP 6)
SPONSON (STEP 5)
BOAT BOOM (STEP 6)

PART 1, STEPS 5 & 6

STERN C/L

PART 1, STEP 7

FLIGHT DECK CUT-OUTS
INSCRIBED LINE

PART 2, STEP 2

PART 2 - FLIGHT DECK: BEFORE

PART 2 - FLIGHT DECK - AFTER

6 GUN 20mm TUB — MAKE 1
2 GUN 20mm TUB — MAKE 2

SPLINTER SHIELDS ARE 2mm HIGH

PART 2, STEP 4

A) INSCRIBE
B) REMOVE

PART 2, STEP 6

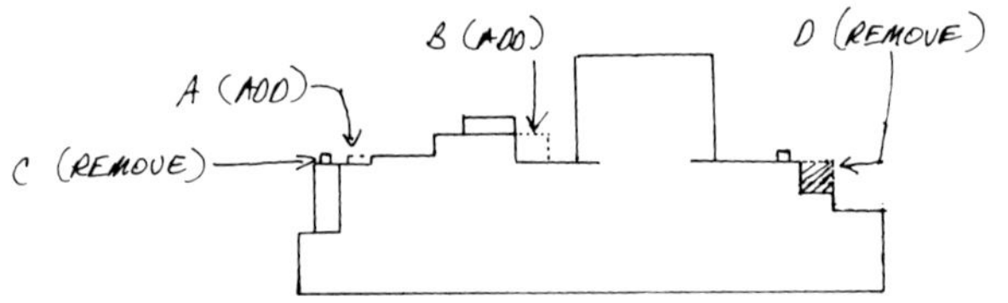

PART 3, STEP 1

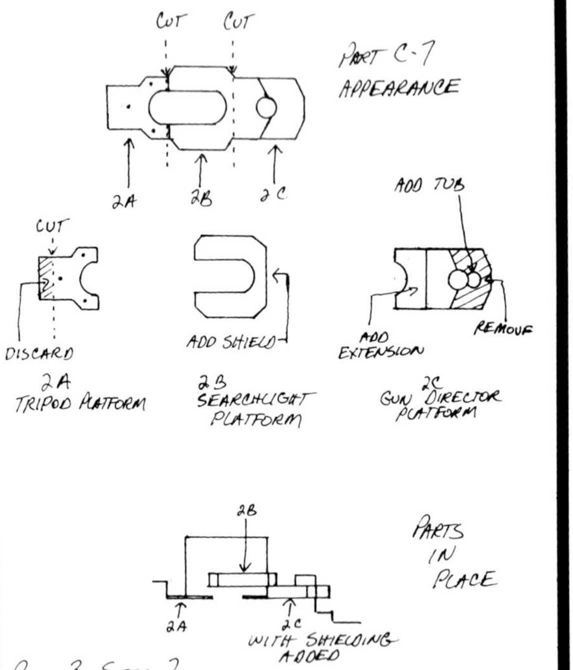

PART 3, STEP 2

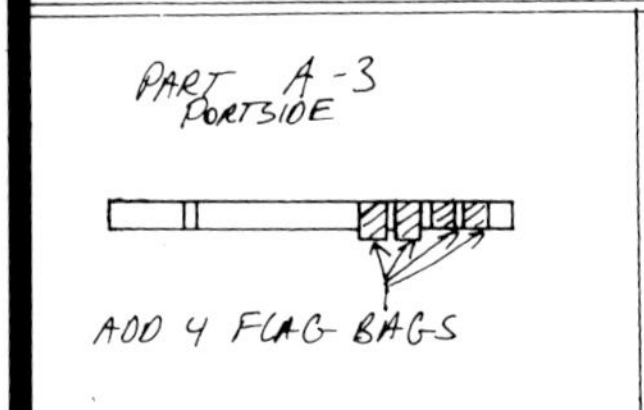

PART 3, STEP 3

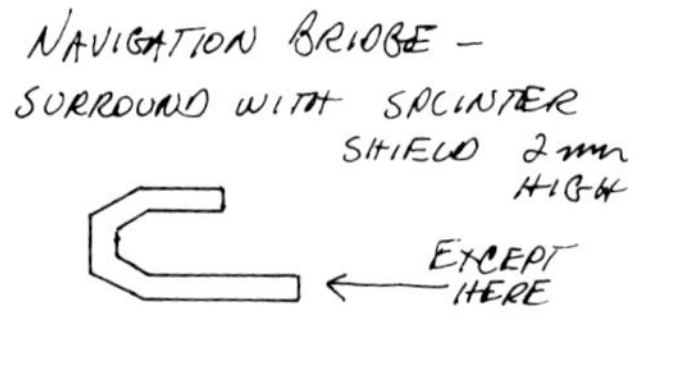

PART 3, STEP 5

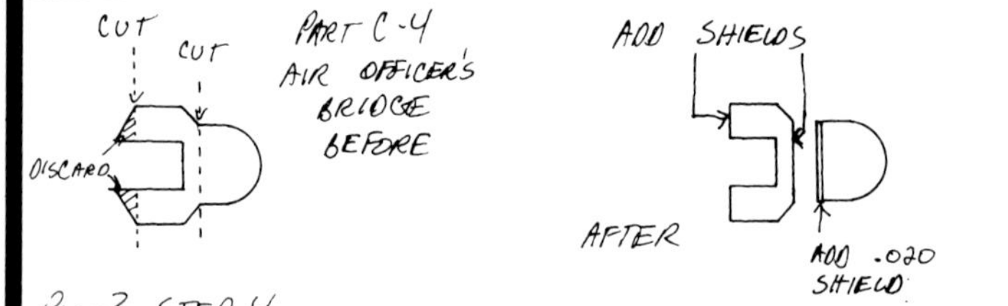

PART 3, STEP 4

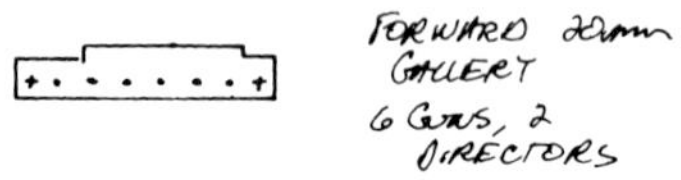

PART 3, STEP 7

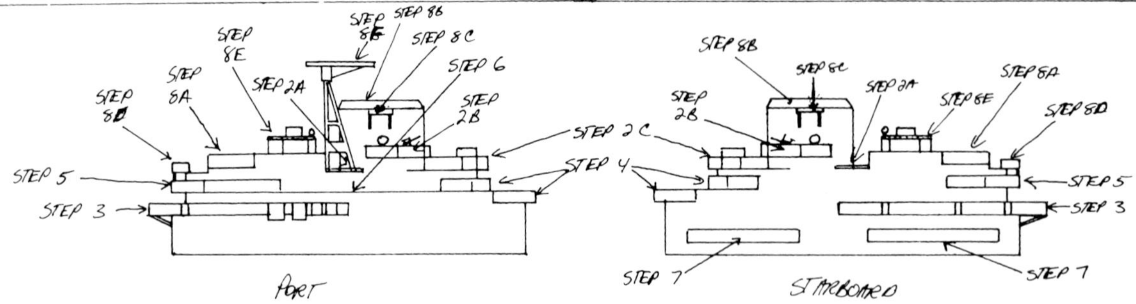

PART 4, ALL CORRECTIONS UP TO STEP 8F MADE

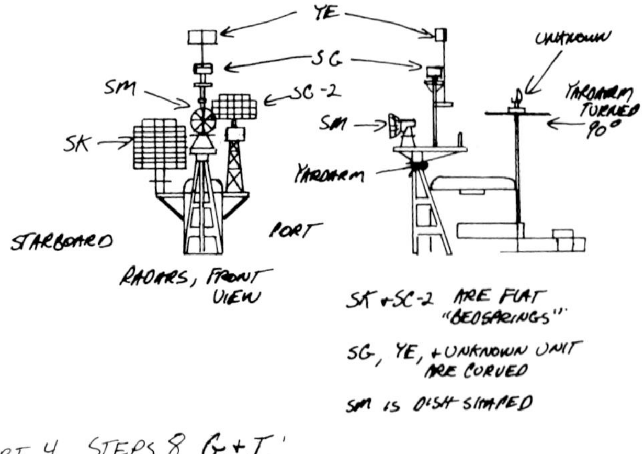

PART 4, STEPS 8 G + I

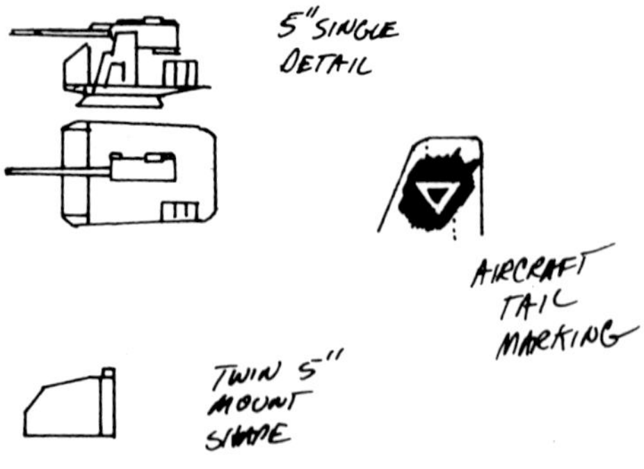

PART 5 (NOT TO SCALE)

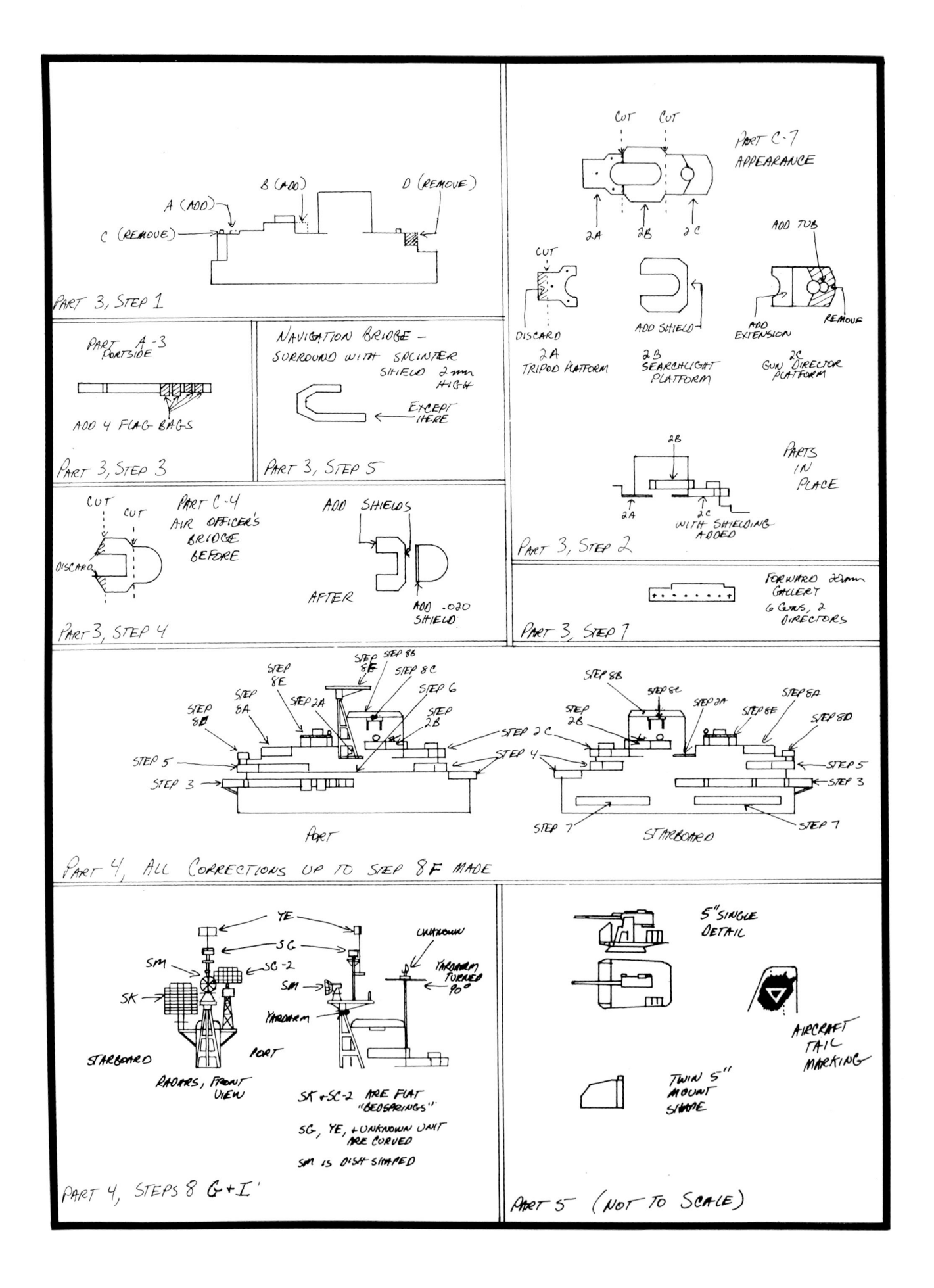

and attach it to the hull. A director tub can be cut from a piece of sprue. The supports for each can be formed from plastic sheet and putty.

Once all of this has been done, most of the hull-related pieces can be installed. I would not install the three 40mm tubs and sponsons to the starboard side below the island at this time since these will interfere with filling the gap between the hull and the flight deck later.

PART 2, CORRECTIONS TO THE FLIGHT DECK

Step 1. A number of sections of catwalks have to be removed from the edges of the flight deck. On the port side, remove the aft stairs leading to the aft five-inch gun gallery, the piece right aft of it that represents the LSO platform, and an 8mm long section of catwalk aft, another section 5mm long from the end of the catwalk next to the location of the "A" five-inch gun mount, and a 20mm long section beginning 7mm aft of the front edge. All of this is illustrated in the "before" and "after" drawings of the flight deck that are included.

Step 2. From the flight deck itself, small trapezoidal sections must be removed from the vicinity of the port 40mm tubs which were repositioned in Part 1. I cut mine up to the inscribed line that represents the edge of the deck planking.

Step 3. This concerns the port side 20mm galleries. (A) Remove the seven-gun gallery abaft the elevator and the foremost six-gun gallery, then switch them around. (B) Remove the eight-gun gallery forward of the elevator, cut it down to the size of the six-gun gallery, and relocate it 10mm forward so that its front edge begins right where the flight deck finishes widening to the left. Don't forget to patch up the holes in the catwalks with strips of .010 sheet plastic.

Step 4. Build three new 20mm gun galleries: one six-gun gallery, and two two-gun tubs. The six-gun tub goes into the 20mm long gap on the starboard side forward. The two two-gun tubs go into the 8mm gaps right aft, to port and starboard. The LSO platform that was removed can be relocated in the space forward of the portside tub. At this point, you can also add the Part D-36, 40mm gun tub on the port side aft.

Step 5. Add two radio mast stubs to the starboard side catwalk edges. One goes just forward of the aftermost two-gun 20mm tub, and the other goes at the end of the catwalk by the "A" five-inch gun mount. LEXINGTON still had the original five radio masts at this time. The kit provides only four, so you must either build a new one or hit the parts box.

Step 6. (A) On the port side of the "box" forward of the "C" five-inch mount, inscribe a rolling door. (B) Take the four Part D-21, platforms, and modify them according to the plan, then attach them. (C) Cut off the little nub that represents a 40mm director tub from atop the "box" by the "C" five-inch gun mount.

Step 7. Several 40mm director tubs were located along the deck edges. Find a piece of round sprue 3mm in diameter and cut off nine 2mm long pieces. Six of these are located along the edges of the port catwalk in the following locations: two abaft the 40mm gun by the forward five-inch gun gallery, one forward of the second 20mm gun gallery, one forward of the Part D-36 40mm gun tub, one abaft the aftermost 20mm gallery, and one between the two aftermost 40mm tubs. On the starboard catwalk, one goes above and a bit forward of the aftermost hangar deck 40mm tub and another just after the aftermost 20mm gallery. The ninth director replaces the one atop the "box" on the flight deck forward of the "C" five-inch gun mount. The deck edge tubs should be fitted so that their tops do not project above the catwalk edges.

Step 8. You can now cement the deck to the hull. Make sure that the gap between the deck and hull below the island's location is filled and sanded down.

Finally, you can add the elevators, radio masts, and any other parts associated with the flight deck or hull that have not yet been installed. If you choose to install the 20mm guns along the flight deck edges now, their arrangement is as follows from fore to aft: port side, 7-6-6-6-2; starboard side, 6-5-10-2.

PART 3, CORRECTIONS TO THE ISLAND STRUCTURE

Step 1. First assemble the two island halves, Parts C-10 and C-11. Little needs to be done to this basic structure. (A) The little step upon which the Part D-41, gun tub, will rest must be extended forward by 2mm, so it will be flush with the front edge of the tub. (B) The box upon which the Part D-19, gun director base, will sit must be extended aft by 3mm. (C) The little nub that represents the forward 40mm director should be removed. (D) A notch 3mm deep by 2mm long has to be removed just aft of the locator pin for the Part C-7, searchlight platform. Fill the resulting hole.

Step 2. Part C-7 represents the searchlight platform and a gun director base as one unit, when they should be on separate levels. Make two cuts that will divide this part into three sections. Part 2A, which will support the tripod mast, must be trimmed to fit between the funnel and the Step 1B extension. Part 2C, the gun director base, needs to be trimmed down and also extended as the plans show, then have the splinter shields added to it. This must fit between the after part of the funnel and the locator pin. A 40mm director tub hangs from the director base overlooking the gun tub below it. Part 2B, the searchlight platform, needs only to have a splinter shield added across the aft edge before putting it into place. You will need to find the searchlights and a couple of 20mm guns in the parts box.

Step 3. Since the 40mm tub does not have to be removed from Part A-3, flag bridge, the only work that needs to be done is the addition of four flag bags on the port side aft.

69

Step 4. The Part C-4, air officer's bridge, needs to have the 40mm tub separated from it. Once accomplished, lay an .020 sheet bulkhead across the open end of the gun tub and position it upon its step on the after island. You may have to fiddle a bit with the molded braces beneath it. Now square off the angled edge of the air officer's bridge and position .010 sheet splinter shields across only the after and starboard edges. Leave the port edge open. This remodeled piece fits into the notch cut in Step 1D.

Step 5. The only major omission is that of a navigation bridge. Fortunately, this can be easily constructed. Surround it with a 2mm high splinter shield, except for the aft port edge. Fit it into place above the flag bridge and on the same level as the air officer's bridge in Step 5. Be sure of this, or you will have problems in the next step.

Step 6. A catwalk connects the navigation and air officer's bridges along the port side of the island. This explains the need for the open edges and accurate placements in Steps 4 and 5. The catwalk need only be only a 2mm wide strip of .020 sheet, and it is unshielded.

Step 7. Of the two 20mm galleries, Part D-42 can be discarded as too small. Instead, trim down the tab on Part C-8 and fit that in its place. Build a new forward gallery to replace Part C-8. This new gallery has five guns like C-8, but instead of just one 40mm director (represented by the large round peg) the new one has two directors, one at each end.

Step 8. A good deal more work is needed to finally finish off the island structure. At this point you may want to cement it to the deck for easier handling. (A) Cement the Part D-41, 40mm tub, into place forward. (B) Remove the projections from the Part C-5, funnel cap, and cement it to the stack. (C) Platforms project from either side of the upper funnel upon which the radars will be mounted. These platforms are braced from the funnel by tubular supports which can be made from stretched sprue or wire. (D) A 40mm director tub overhangs, and is braced upon, the navigation bridge. (E) The Part D-19, gun director platform, should actually be an open structure surrounding the gun director base. It can be hollowed out with careful cutting and sawing. Once it is in place, a piece of sprue can be positioned in it to serve as the gun director base. (F) Remove the raised ridges and yardarms from the Part D-32, radar platform. Cement it to the tripod. (G) A pole mainmast needs to be fitted abaft the funnel. (H) To my mind, the Part 48, gun directors, and their Part D-38, radars, are rather sad looking. I replaced them with spares from the parts box. (I) The radar array is the last item to be fitted. On the starboard platform goes the big SK bedspring, while the SC-2 is raised up on a lattice mast to port. On the foremast, the SM dominates the fore end, with an SG and a YE beacon raised up high abaft it. A radar that I could not identify tops the main mast. My gear came from the parts box or was made from bits and pieces of scrap plastic. Photoetched parts for the radars are also available.

PART 4, FINISHING TOUCHES

My finishing touches were limited to just a few more bits of work. I added simulated bracing beneath all of the new areas of catwalk and the bridge with thin slivers of .010 sheet. The five-inch single mounts had working platforms and fuse setters added. The five-inch twin mounts are badly undersized, so I sawed them in half lengthwise and added an .020 shim before cementing the halves together. When dry, I then cut them apart widthwise and added another .020 shim. When this had dried, they were sanded to shape, the gun barrels were added, and white glue was worked in to simulate the "bloomers" in the mount openings. More ambitious modelers may want to go further, but this was enough to satisfy me for now. Some further possibilities will be presented in Part 7.

PART 5, PAINTING

LEXINGTON went through the war until her final 1945 refit in the Measure 21 system. Simply put, all vertical surfaces were painted in 5N Navy Blue. The flight deck was stained with the Norfolk N-250 blue stain, while the metal decks were painted with the matching 20-B Deck Blue paint. The flight deck markings were limited to the three sets of dashed lines and the hull number fore and aft. These were apparently painted in Dull Black. Paints in these colors once were, and possibly still are, available from the Floating Drydock, but instead, I used homebrews of PollyS paints to match their camouflage chip card. They might not be exact, but once you have finished adding rust, grime, and weathering, it doesn't matter if it is a little off.

PART 6, AIRCRAFT

Except for the F4U Corsairs, the aircraft provided with the kit can be painted to represent Air Group 19 which was on board in October 1944. For that period, the TBMs and the SB2Cs had the three color scheme of Sea Blue uppersurfaces blending in to Intermediate Blue sides, which blended into white undersurfaces. The SB2Cs also had the folding panels of the wings' undersurfaces in Intermediate Blue. The F6Fs were in overall Gloss Sea Blue, but a few of the tricolor schemes may still have been on board. The gloss of the colors faded quickly to flat with exposure to the sun and sea, so I used the appropriate PollyS flat colors. National markings were the standard white star and bar with the blue disc and outline in four positions (both sides of the fuselage, top of left wing, and bottom of right wing), but the F6Fs omitted the disc and outline. LEXINGTON's aircraft at that time were identified by a hollow triangle, apex down, painted in white on their tails, though the F6Fs did not carry this marking.

PART 7, FURTHER POSSIBILITIES

As mentioned previously, there is much more work that can be done. The 40mm quad shapes are not quite right; the 20mm guns might be slimmed down and have the slits cut in their shields; steam pipes and loudspeakers can be added to the island. These are just a few things that come to mind right now.

I had received a note from Bert McDowell, whose model of HORNET (CV-12), (for which he used this same kit) had won a first place award in the ships category at the 1986 IPMS National Convention in Sacramento. I asked him if he would mind relating a few tips on what he might have done to his model. His comments, somewhat edited, follow:

"The major operation to me was the flight deck. It isn't thick enough to accommodate the gallery deck, and HORNET only had a single catapult. I ground off all of the deckhouses and sanded down the relief on the deck until I was sure that no lumps would show through the rather thin .020 scribed sheet I would apply on top of it. Then I traced the deck outline onto the scribed sheet. You must cut the overlay a bit long so you can shape the rounddowns at the ends of the deck. The width should also be slightly oversized too. You come back with a square sanding block, sanding to smooth the edge and fill between the deck and overlay. You will have to replace the blocks for the second and third five-inch mounts and the 40mm quad, but it is worth it. You now have complete control over all the deck detailing."

"Before final assembly, I added railing all over the ship. This and other details like radars were from an etched brass sheet available from Tom's Modelworks (USN Carrier # 1). I also added some gallery detail to the underside of the deck as per the plans in Roberts' Anatomy of the Ship: USS INTREPID."

That is all I have on building the LEXINGTON in her 1944 configuration. As with the articles I have written, I welcome any and all comments and criticisms that would be helpful. I can be reached at 98 Grayson Street, Staten Island, NY 10306.

POST-CONVERSION MODELS

We will approach modeling the LEXINGTON in her post-modernization configuration differently than we did for the World War II model. Space does not permit an item-by-item description of how to build one of the two available kits into a model of the LEXINGTON. Instead, in this segment of the Modelers Section, we will basically review the two kits that might be used as a starting point for the modernized LEXINGTON. After choosing one of these kits, the modeler has the extensive detailed photographs of this book to direct his effort. As was the case with the World War II model, a specific time frame will have to be chosen, since details of the ship have changed between her recommissioning in 1955 and the present. Most noticeable of these are the changes in the radar fit and the gradual but continuous reduction in armament until it was all finally deleted. Other changes, such as the addition of the life rafts to the gun sponsons, catapult extensions, modifications to the numbers 1 and 2 elevators, and reduction in arresting gear also need to be noted. Because of this, in our section on the modernized LEXINGTON, we have made a special effort to date the photographs and point out the changes that were made to the ship as she went through yard periods. With this information, and with the numerous detailed photographs that begin on page 42, modelers will have sufficient information from which to build an accurate model of the LEXINGTON after her SCB-27C/-125 modernization.

Revell 1/540th Scale Kit

The older of the two kits that can be used to build a modernized LEXINGTON is the Revell kit, which is in 1/540th scale. It was first released as the ESSEX, and has since been re-released as WASP, HORNET, BON HOMME RICHARD, and even LEXINGTON herself. These re-releases differed only in decals offered, catapult extensions, and types of aircraft included. This kit is a good news--bad news situation. The good news is that, considering its thirty-year age, it is an excellent kit. It is well done, nicely detailed, and is still generally available. The bad news is that it does not represent the LEXINGTON at any time since her modernization. It is a fairly accurate representation of an ESSEX class carrier that had the SCB-27A/-125 modernization. It has the hydraulic catapults and the single five-inch gun on the starboard quarter, rather than the sponson with two five-inch mounts and a twin three-inch mount such as was installed on LEXINGTON. The kit can be built into a reasonably good model of the ESSEX, WASP, HORNET, or BENNINGTON, for example, as they appeared right after their modernizations. It could not be used for any of the SCB-27C/-125 modernizations without extensive rework.

There are some shortcomings that should be mentioned. The bridge area is totally incorrect and must be rebuilt regardless of which ship is modeled. The propellers don't look like the real thing at all; there is no hangar deck, nor is there a gallery deck hanging below the flight deck. The hull is too narrow, and this is most noticeable at the escalator on the starboard side. The portion below the flight deck does not line up with the part on the starboard side of the island. The guns, particularly the five-inchers, are not very accurate, and the one on the starboard quarter is located at the flight deck level instead of being just below it as it should be. The forward elevator is rectangular in shape, rather than being the enlarged version, which, for the LEXINGTON issue, Revell tried to cover with a decal outline that attempted to make the elevator look more like the present number 1 elevator. The bow below the waterline is incorrect, not having the bulbous shape it requires.

Much work would have to be done to make this kit look like LEXINGTON at any point in time. The hurricane bow would have to be completely reshaped, and the vertical facings on each side of the bow just below the flight deck

The Revell LEXINGTON in 1/540th scale is really a re-release of a re-release of a re-release. It represents the ESSEX as she was modernized, and this varies considerably from the LEXINGTON. This model could also be used to build a WASP or HORNET after modernization, but it would take a lot of work to get it to look like LEXINGTON. It can be done though if one is willing to put in the work. It is a better model than the Renwal model as far as detailing is concerned.

level would have to be added to replace the existing catwalks. The starboard quarter gun sponson would have to be added, and the rest of the gun armament would have to be altered to fit the appropriate time frame. While the kit simply is not LEXINGTON, one good thing about Revell's issuing it as this ship is that they included T-28s and T-2s, which have operated from the carrier since she assumed her role as the Navy's training carrier. The T-28s no longer operate from the LEXINGTON, but the T-2s do. The Phantoms are totally wrong for any ESSEX class carrier.

While it would take a skilled modeler many hours to turn this kit into a model of the LEXINGTON, it could be done. With the scarcity of the Renwal kit, this may be the only kit that many modelers can find today that could be used to build a modernized ESSEX. To list all of the changes that would have to be made would fill many pages, but the kit is basically a good one, and the result may be well worth the effort.

Renwal 1/500th Scale Kit

The biggest problem with this kit is that it has become very hard to find. It is no longer generally available, and must be found by shopping sales by collectors or modelers with older kits to sell. It was issued as the SHANGRI-LA, and, since SHANGRI-LA and LEXINGTON were modernized together, receiving both the SCB-27C and SCB-125 modernizations simultaneously, their features are very much alike. Therefore, straight from the box, this kit more closely resembles LEXINGTON right after her recommissioning than does the Revell kit.

Unfortunately, this is not as good a kit as the Revell model. Below the waterline it is absolutely awful, and this means that the modeler is faced with a choice between MAJOR surgery or a simpler solution of building a waterline model. The flight deck landing lines are scribed on and raised, and will have to be sanded off. We would recommend sanding the flight deck completely smooth and starting over by adding the detail yourself anyway. The wedge shaped area ahead of the port elevator is

The Renwal model of the SHANGRI-LA in 1/500th scale more accurately represents the way LEXINGTON appeared right after her recommissioning than does the Revell model. However, it does not have the nice detailing that the Revell kit has, and is really poor below the waterline. It too will take a lot of work to turn it into a good model of the LEXINGTON.

present as it was on the SHANGRI-LA and LEXINGTON right after their modernizations. The bridge area is bad, the doors on the island stand far too proud, the waterline is scribed into the hull, is too high, and must be removed. A hangar deck must be added, and a great deal more work must be done. The model is not as well detailed as the Revell kit, so detailing must be added to suit the modeler. Most noticeable is the lack of framing and support members under various sections of flight deck overhang.

On the plus side, the shape of the bow and its vertical facings are more nearly correct for LEXINGTON as well as SHANGRI-LA and BON HOMME RICHARD. The life rafts that were present when the ship was recommissioned are included, while they are not in the Revell kit. In either case, the ones used today would have to be built from scratch if LEXINGTON were to be modeled as she now appears. The gun armament is no better than the Revell kit, and should be built from scratch if needed for a model during the time frame when the LEXINGTON carried guns.

As with the Revell kit, the Renwal model will require a lot of work to build a post-modernization LEXINGTON, but it can be done. Careful study of the photographs in this book, a lot of patient work, and application of good modeling skills and techniques will result in a decent model of the ship.

SUMMARY

The simplest model of a modernized LEXINGTON would be to use the Renwal kit to build a waterline model of the ship as she appeared right after her modernization. This would require the least amount of major changes. We believe that the Renwal kit would also be marginally better than the Revell kit for building the LEXINGTON in any of her post-modernization configurations simply because it was based on the SHANGRI-LA which shared common features with LEXINGTON. The Revell kit is definitely the better of the two, but it was based on the ESSEX, and there are many major differences between the ESSEX and LEXINGTON. Either way it will be a real job. Aircraft from the Revell issue as the LEXINGTON will be helpful regardless of which kit is used. The only other way to build a modernized LEXINGTON is to build it from scratch!